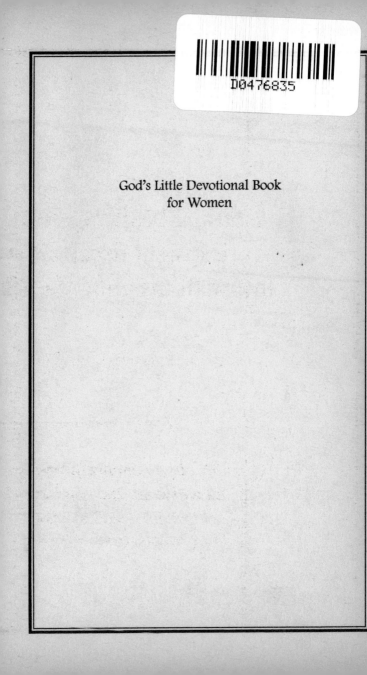

God's Little Devotional Book
for Women

God's Little
Devotional Book
for Women

eagle

Guildford, Surrey

Scripture quotations used within this book is as follows:
AMP – *Amplified Bible*
AV – *Authorised Version*
GNB – *Good News Bible*, © Bible Society
JBP – *J.B. Phillips*, © Fontana Books, 1960
NASB – *The New American Standard Bible*, © The Lockman Foundation, 1960, 1962, 1963, 1968, 1971, 1972, 1973, 1975, 1977.
NIV – *New International Version* © Hodder & Stoughton
NJK – *New King James* © Thomas Nelson
RSV and NRSV – *Revised Standard Version*, © Division of Christian Education of the National Council of the Churches of Christ in the USA.
TLB – *The Living Bible*, © Tyndale House, 1971

Printed in Great Britain by Cox & Wyman Ltd, Reading, Berks.
ISBN: 0 86347 273 7

Introduction

The devotionals in this book have been selected to provide a pick-me-up for your day. In the same way a snack or drink gives you a burst of physical energy, these devotionals are snacks for the soul, awakening you to new insights about yourself and your relationships with family, friends and colleagues. They will encourage you in your daily walk with God and will serve as a source of motivation as you accomplish your goals and fulfil your dreams.

Our hope is that the material in this book will remind you of God's promise – He is always near. Whether your heart is crying for comfort, protection, an expanded outlook, or direction, through these pages you will see He is both willing and eager to draw you closer to Himself, shield you from harm, comfort you with His presence, and encourage you with His Word.

Do you need a pick-me-up today? Then these devotionals are for you!

My job is to take care
of the possible
and trust God with
the impossible

*Those who know your name will trust in
you, for you, LORD, have never forsaken
those who seek you.*
Psalm 9:10 NIV

Dr Amanda Whitworth was frustrated as she crept up a hill with eight cars in front of her. They were stuck behind a slow-moving truck, and she was in a hurry. Amanda's last patient had needed more attention than was allotted for regular examinations and she was late leaving to pick up her daughter from school. Now she breathed a prayer that she would not be late again. It would be her third time, and because the school did not tolerate parental tardiness, she would have to make new arrangements for Allie's afternoon care.

Amanda silently fumed at the truck's progress. No one dared pass the truck on the long hill, as it was impossible to see oncoming cars around it. Suddenly, the truck driver waved his hand indicating that all was clear ahead. As Amanda zipped past him, it occurred to her that this man was probably a stranger to all who passed him – yet nine people trusted their lives and the lives of their families to this man.

What a tremendous picture of how we do all we can do and then must trust even the smallest details of our lives to the care of God – who is a loving Heavenly Father. And how comforting to know he can always see exactly what's ahead!

When Mother Teresa
received her Nobel Prize,
she was asked,
'What can we do to
promote world peace?'
She replied, 'Go home and
love your family'.

Let love and faithfulness never leave you;
bind them around your neck, write them
on the tablet of your heart.
Proverbs 3.3 NIV

'The family,' says Mother Teresa, 'is the place to learn about Jesus. God has sent the family – together as husband and wife and children – to be His love.'

In *Words to Love By . . .* , Mother Teresa writes, 'Once a lady came to me in great sorrow and told me that her daughter had lost her husband and a child. All the daughter's hatred had turned on the mother. She wouldn't even see the mother.

'So I said, "Now you think a bit about the things that your daughter liked when she was a child. Maybe flowers or a special food. Try to give her some of these things without looking for a return."

'And she started doing some of these things, like putting the daughter's favourite flower on the table, or leaving a beautiful piece of cloth for her. And she did not look for a return from the daughter.

'Several days later the daughter said, "Mummy, come. I love you. I want you."

'It was very beautiful.

'By being reminded of the joy of childhood, the daughter reconnected with her family life. She must have had a happy childhood to go back to the joy and happiness of her mother's love.'[1]

You are never so high as when you are on your knees

Humble yourselves in the sight of the Lord, and he shall lift you up.

James 4:10 AV

On a stormy day, with two experienced guides, a woman climbed the Weisshorn in the Swiss Alps. As they neared the peak, the woman – exhilarated by the view before her – sprang forward and was almost blown away by a gust of wind. One of the guides caught her and pulled her down, saying 'On your knees, madam! You are safe here only on your knees.'

We typically regard 'on our knees' as the standard position for prayer, but talking to God isn't limited to any position. He can hear us . . . regardless.

Three Christian women were talking once about the 'best' position for prayer. One argued the importance of holding one's hands together and pointing them upwards. The second advocated that prayer was best when one was stretched out on the floor. The third thought standing was better than kneeling. As they talked, a telephone repairman listened as he worked on a nearby phone system. Finally, he could contain himself no longer and interjected, 'I have found that the post powerful prayer I ever made was while I was dangling upside down from a power pole, suspended 40 feet above the ground.'

The important thing is not your *position* of prayer, but the fact that you do pray!

Give your troubles
to God:
He will be up all
night anyway.

He will not allow your foot to slip;
He who keeps you will not slumber.
Psalm 121:3 NASB

Why pray? We pray because prayer opens up the floodgates of God's infinite grace and power to flow toward the person in need. God can act without prayer, but He chooses to operate within the boundaries of human will and invitation. He allows us to participate in His work on earth with each prayer.

Leonard Ravenhill once said about prayer, 'One might estimate the weight of the world, tell the size of the celestial city, count the stars of heaven, measure the speed of lightning and tell the time of the rising and the setting of the sun – but you cannot estimate prayer power. Prayer is as vast as God because He is behind it. Prayer is as mighty as God because He has committed Himself to answer it.'

A sign in a cotton factory read: 'If your threads get tangled, send for the foreman.' One day a new worker got her threads tangled. The more she tried to disentangle them, the worse the situation grew. Finally, she sent for the foreman. He asked, 'Why didn't you send for me earlier?' She replied. 'I was doing my best.' He answered, 'No, your best would have been to send for me.'

When we face a tough situation, our first response should be to ask for God's help. He longs to be our helper and to be fully involved in our lives.

We should seize
every opportunity to
give encouragement.
Encouragement is
oxygen to the soul.

Everyone enjoys giving good advice, and
how wonderful it is to be able to say the
right thing at the right time!
Proverbs 15:23 TLB

In *Especially for a Woman*,[2] Ann Kiemel Anderson writes in her unique style about her sister: 'Jan taught 3rd grade once. a long time ago. One bright-eyed boy would stand at her desk. Watch her. talk to her. All the while wrapping his finger around a piece of her hair into a little curl. He thought Jan was the shining star in the night. Over & over, however, he did poorly in his work assignments & daily quizzes.

'One day Jan stopped, looked at him, & said, "Rodney, you are very smart. You could be doing so well in school. In fact, you are one of my finest students . . ." Before she could continue to tell him that he should be doing much better in school . . . he looked up at her with sober, large eyes:

"I did not know that!"

'From that moment on, Rodney began to change. His papers were neater. cleaner, his spelling improved. He was one of her top students. all because she affirmed him. She told him something no one ever had before. It changed his life.'

Nobody ever became ill or died from receiving too much genuine praise and encouragement. But who can count the wounded hearts, weary souls and troubled minds that have resulted from their lack!

You may give
without loving,
but you cannot love
without giving.

*For God so loved the world that he gave
his only Son, that whoever believes in him
should not perish but have eternal life.*
John 3:16 RSV

Most authorities believe King David's temple was built on Mount Moriah where Abraham was told to sacrifice Isaac. But there's another Hebrew legend that presents a different story.

The legend says that two brothers lived on adjoining farms which were divided from the peak to the base of the mountain. The younger brother lived alone, unmarried. The older brother had a large family.

One night during grain harvest, the older brother awoke and thought, *My brother is all alone. To cheer his heart, I will take some of my sheaves and lay them on his side of the field.*

At the same hour, the younger brother awoke and thought, *My brother has a large family and greater needs than I do. As he sleeps, I'll put some of my sheaves on his side of the field.* Each brother went out carrying sheaves to the other's field and met halfway. When they declared their intentions to each other, they dropped their sheaves and embraced. It is at that place, the legend claims, the temple was built.

Whether or not this story is true, it exemplifies the best expression of love – *giving*. Giving is one of life's best relation-builders.

When I come to the end of
my rope, God is there
to take over.

*. . . for He Himself has said, 'I will never
leave you nor forsake you.'*
Hebrews 13:5 NKJ

The end of our human abilities is our opportunity to turn to God. But giving up our independence to depend on God isn't necessarily easy. We are often like the woman in this story reported in the *Los Angeles Times*:

A screaming woman, trapped in a car dangling from a freeway transition road in East Los Angeles, was rescued Saturday morning . . . A half dozen passing motorists stopped, grabbed some ropes from one of the vehicles, tied the ropes to the back of the woman's car, and hung on until the fire units arrived. A ladder was extended from below to help stabilise the car while fire-fighters tied the vehicle to tow trucks with cables and chains.

'Every time we would move the car,' said one rescuer, 'she'd yell and scream. She was in pain.'

It took almost two and a half hours for the passersby, CHP officers, towtruck drivers and fire-fighters – about 25 people in all – to secure the car and pull the woman to safety.

'It was kinda funny,' LA County Fire Capt. Ross Marshall recalled later. 'She kept saying, "I'll do it myself".'[3]

The Lord can do
great things
through those
who don't care
who gets the credit

A man's pride shall bring him low: but
honour shall uphold the humble in spirit.
Proverbs 29:23 AV

Until the time Jane learned she needed an operation, the question, 'Who will take care of me if I get sick?' had only been hypothetical. As a single woman, she hadn't given much thought to how she would survive a major illness or operation. As it turned out, she found that she had a 'loving menagerie of friends' who 'cobbled together a schedule of ministry and then passed the baton from one to the next while I marvelled at my good fortune.'[4]

Stephanie was the ringmaster, the one by her side at the hospital, who also helped her check her incision and take showers. Bob drove up from Los Angeles with his dog to stay for a few days after she returned home. Peggy brought over Thai take-away food. Ann arrived with a bread machine and bags of groceries. She also made soup, mopped the kitchen floor and did the laundry. Michelle brought mail from the office and drove her to doctor's appointments.

It was amazing to Jane that these various people hardly knew each other when they first began helping her, but by the time she recovered, they had all become friends.

Being a servant has wonderful rewards. Many times in our serving we receive much more than we ever give away.

What sunshine is to flowers,
smiles are to humanity.
They are but trifles,
to be sure but, scattered
along life's pathway,
the good they do is
inconceivable.

A happy heart makes the face cheerful
Proverbs 15:13 NIV

The practice of one particular church was to dismiss the children in the Sunday morning service just prior to the sermon. The children would all march forward in a makeshift processional and sing a song as they passed the pulpit on their way to hear a sermon prepared just for them. The pastor enjoyed this part of the service. He made it a point to smile at each child and to receive a smile in return.

To his surprise, one morning, a curly-headed four-year-old girl ran out of the procession and threw herself into her mother's arms, sobbing deeply. The pastor sought out the mother after the service to see what had happened. The child had told her, 'I smiled at God, but He didn't smile back.'

The pastor's heart sank. He had failed to smile and her joy had turned to torment.

We may think our smiles do not represent God to another person, but they just might! Genuine smiles are a sign of affirmation, appreciation and love.

Your smile can bring hope and change the countenance of someone today. Give it a try!

I regret often that
I have spoken;
never that
I have been silent.

In the multitude of words there
wanteth not sin: but he that
refraineth his lips is wise.
Proverbs 10:19 AV

When Western Union asked Thomas Edison to 'name his price' for the telegraph he had invented, he asked for several days to consider it. His wife suggested $20,000 but he thought such an amount was exorbitant.

At the appointed time he went to the meeting still unsure as to his sales price. When the official asked, 'How much?' He tried to say $20,000, but the words just wouldn't come out of his mouth. The official finally broke the silence and asked, 'Well, how about $100,000?'

Often silence allows others to say something better than we could have said it ourselves! By keeping quiet, others will have a greater interest in our thoughts . . . then when we have an interested audience, our words will have greater impact.

The Bible tells us that even a fool may be thought of as wise when his mouth is kept shut (Proverbs 17:28). In that sense, silence can keep us from embarrassing ourselves. People may think we are smarter than we really are!

When you feel moved to express an opinion, weigh the impact of your words and keep this thought in mind. 'The *less* said, the *best* said.' We can't get in trouble for what we don't say! Like Edison, we might even benefit from our silence.

'I can forgive, but I cannot forget,' is only another way of saying, 'I will not forgive.' Forgiveness ought to be like a cancelled note – torn in two, and burned up, so that it never can be shown against one.

Be kind to each other, be compassionate. Be as ready to forgive others as God for Christ's sake has forgiven you.
Ephesians 4:32 JBP

A man once had too much to drink at a party. First, he made a foolish spectacle of himself – even to the point of wearing the proverbial lampshade as a hat – and then he passed out. Friends helped his wife take him home and put him to bed. The next morning he was very remorseful and asked his wife to forgive him. She agreed to 'forgive and forget' the incident.

As the months went by, however, the wife referred to the incident from time to time, always with a little note of ridicule and shame in her voice. Finally, the man grew weary of being reminded of his bad behaviour and said, 'I thought you were going to forgive and forget.'

'I have forgiven and forgotten,' the wife argued, 'but I just don't want you to forget that I have forgiven and forgotten.'

Once we have confronted the offender, we must remember nothing is gained from harbouring unforgiveness in our hearts. Forgiveness requires a healing process inside us – to the point where we no longer feel any pain at the memory of what the other person did or said to injure us.

We 'forget' when we no longer hurt! When you make a commitment to forgive another person, ask the Lord to heal you of the impact of that person's behaviour on your life. Forgive, forget and start living again.

Worry is like a
rocking chair: it gives you
something to do,
but doesn't get you
anywhere.

*Casting the whole of your care – all your
anxieties, all your worries, all your concerns, once and for all – on Him; for He
cares for you affectionately, and cares
about you watchfully.*
1 Peter 5:7 AMP

People who continually worry about every detail of their lives are like a patient in a mental hospital who stood with her ear pressed against the wall.

'What are you doing?' an attendant asked with curiosity.

'Shhh,' the woman whispered, beckoning to the attendant to join her at the wall.

The attendant pressed her ear to the wall and stood there for several moments listening intently. 'I can't hear anything,' she said.

'No,' the patient replied with a furrowed brow. 'It's been like that all day!'

Some worry about what might be said. Others worry about what hasn't been said. Some worry about what might happen. Others worry about what hasn't happened which should have happened by now. Others worry about their future while others fret over the consequences of their past.

We were created to live abundant lives in our mind, our body and our spirit. Like a flower we were meant to blossom, not to wither on the vine. Put Jesus in charge of your worries today and walk in newness of life!

Look around you and
be distressed,
Look within you and
be depressed,
Look to Jesus and
be at rest.

*In my distress I cried unto the LORD,
and he heard me.*
Psalm 120:1 AV

The 911 emergency system has amazing capabilities. In most places in the United States, a person need only dial those three numbers to be instantly connected to a dispatcher. On a computer screen the dispatcher instantly see the caller's telephone number, address and the name under which the number is listed. Also listening in on the call are police, fire and paramedic assistants. A caller need not say anything once the call is made. Even rasping coughs and hysterical cries have brought a quick response. The dispatcher knows where the call is coming from and help is sent.

At times, some situations in our lives are so desperate and our pain so deep we can only muster 911 prayers to God. These are called 'SOS' prayers and they often use the same words: 'God, I need help!' God hears each one. He knows our name and every detail of the situation. Like a Heavenly Dispatcher, He will send precisely who is needed to assist us.

Also like a 911 dispatcher, our Heavenly Dispatcher may have some advice to sustain us through a crisis. Keep a listening ear . . . and remember, help is on the way!

There is no greater love
than the love that holds on
where there seems nothing
left to hold on to.

*Love never fails – never fades out or
becomes obsolete or comes to an end.*
1 Corinthians 13:8 AMP

A family sailing trip almost turned into a tragedy when gale-force winds and towering waves threatened to sink their vessel. Their frantic call to the coastguard brought two ships to their rescue. Unfortunately, the first ship had only a rope ladder, a means of evacuation too dangerous in such rough seas. Then the 900-ft tanker, *James N. Sullivan,* arrived. It shielded the sailboat until, after several hours of manoeuvring, a set of stairs could be lowered from the side of the tanker to the sailboat.

Using a tether safety line, Bob and Sherry made the transfer in good order, as did their two young children. Then it was grandmother Laurie's turn. Grandfather Dave passed her tether to Bob, but her harness got caught when she stepped across to the ladder. As the boats pulled apart, Laurie fell into the sea. With a surge of the waves, the boats came crashing back together. Dave was afraid to look – he knew that his beloved wife of thirty-three years could not swim, and even worse, he feared she may have been crushed as the boats collided. Nevertheless, he clung to the tether, refusing to let go. Grandmother later explained, 'That's the only reason I'm here.'

No matter how troubled the seas of life may become, hold on to the tether with your love. A life will be saved because you trusted God for the impossible!

Daily prayers
will diminish
your cares.

Evening, and morning, and at noon,
will I pray, and cry aloud:
and he shall hear my voice.
Psalm 55:17 AV

Many children learn to count on their fingers, but a nurse once taught a child to pray 'on his fingers.'

This was her method:

Your thumb is the digit nearest to your heart, so pray first for those who are closest to you. Your own needs, of course, should be included, as well as those of your beloved family and friends.

The second finger is the one used for pointing. Pray for those who point you towards the truth, whether at church or school. Pray for your teachers, mentors, pastors and those who inspire your faith.

The third finger is the tallest. Let it stand for the leaders in every sphere of life. Pray for those in authority – both within the body of Christ and those who hold office in various areas of government.

The fourth finger is the weakest, as every pianist knows. Let it stand for those who are in trouble and pain – the sick, injured, abused, wounded or hurt.

The little finger is the smallest. Let it stand for those who often go unnoticed, including those who suffer abuse and deprivation.

What a simple and wonderful reminder as we pray! What a great tool to use in teaching children how to pray for themselves and others.

Be like a postage stamp – stick to one thing till you get there

Be steadfast, immovable, always abounding in the work of the Lord, knowing that your toil is not in vain in the Lord.
1 Corinthians 15:58 NASB

All her life, Veronica worked in jobs that served other people but gave her little personal satisfaction. As a young girl, she missed a lot of school to take care of her younger siblings and help with the family business. Consequently, she never learned to read.

After getting married, she worked as a cook in a restaurant, memorising the ingredient labels and recipes to conceal her illiteracy. Every day she lived in fear of making a mistake, while dreaming of one day being able to read.

A serious illness put Veronica in hospital and then at home for a long recovery. Her health improved a little, but not enough for her to go back to work. She saw this time as her opportunity to learn to read and she enrolled in the adult reading programme.

Veronica's new reading skills boosted her confidence and she got involved in her church and in organising community activities. She wrote a prize-winning cookbook and became a local celebrity.

Veronica never let go of her dream while working hard wherever she found herself. In the end, her dreams were realised far beyond her imagination!

A good laugh is
sunshine in a house

*The light in the eyes [of him whose heart
is joyful] rejoices the heart of others*
Proverbs 15:30 AMP

Peggy was nervous about the dinner party she and her husband were about to host. It was their first time to have guests for dinner since the birth of their son, Pete. To top off Peggy's tension, the guests included her husband Bill's new supervisor.

Sensing the tension in his parents, the baby became irritable and 'fussy' which only added to Peggy's frustration. In an attempt to comfort little Pete, Peggy picked him up, raised him high over her head, and kissed his bare tummy. To her surprise, he smiled and giggled – the first genuine laugh she had heard from her young son.

In an instant, the evening took on an entirely new tenor. Peggy became more relaxed, and Baby Pete relaxed as well. The dinner party was a great success.

Can the laughter of a little child change a day? Yes! So can the laughter shared between two adults, or the chuckle prompted by the memory of a funny event.

When you're feeling 'stressed out' don't allow yourself to explode in anger. Get alone if you have to, but find a reason to laugh . . . and watch the stress melt away!

Each loving act says
loud and clear.
'I love you.
God loves you.
I care.
God cares.'

*Beloved, let us love one another: for love is
of God; and every one that loveth is born
of God . . . for God is love.*
1 John 4:7,8 KJV

Awarm-from-the-oven casserole taken to the home of a sick friend . . .

A bouquet of flowers from your garden given to a neighbour . . .

A thank-you note sent to the performers who did such an excellent job during a concert or play you attended . . .

A loaf of freshly baked cinnamon bread brought to the office for coffee break . . .

A box of biscuits taken to the police station on Christmas day to encourage those who are 'on duty' during the holiday . . .

A call to ask with genuine care and concern, 'How are you doing? . . . '

We may not think of these as acts of Christian witnessing, yet they are. *Every* act of loving kindness reflects God's loving kindness for His people. We give because Jesus Christ has so freely given His love to us. He is the example we follow.

Never dismiss an act of loving kindness as being too small or inconsequential. God will magnify even our smallest deeds to reveal His love to others.

I have held many things in
my hands and lost them all;
but the things I have placed
in God's hands,
those I always possess.

I know whom I have believed,
and I am sure that he is able to guard
until that Day what has been
entrusted to me.

2 Timothy 1:12 RSV

Two sisters had held a desire from childhood to one day go to the mission field together. As they approached mid-life, they realised they were both well established in their professions, and they began to investigate where they might go to serve God. After several months of talking to various missionary agencies, one of the sisters quit her job and moved to South America, where she became involved in pioneering churches.

The other sister, however, decided the hazards of the mission field were too great. She would remain at home and make even more money. 'I'll go later,' she said as she bid her sister goodbye. Two years later she died in an accident on the job. She had 'saved' her life . . . only to lose it.

Safety is an illusion apart from God. Many people trust in their jobs – unaware that their companies are on the brink of bankruptcy. Others trust in the government – unaware that funds are diminishing and laws are subject to change. Still others trust in their own abilities, never counting on accidents or illness.

If the Lord has spoken to your heart to 'Go', be swift to respond when He opens the door for you to do so.

A good deed is never lost;
he who sows courtesy
reaps friendship, and
he who plants kindness
gathers love

Whatever a man sows, that he will also reap . . . And let us not grow weary while doing good, for in due season we shall reap if we do not lose heart.

Galatians 6:7,9 NKJ

Joy Sprague knows how to brighten the days of her customers. As the postmistress for Little Cranberry Island, Maine, she actually has customers competing to get their pictures on her post-office wall. Every 25th customer to use the US Postal Service's Express Mail has a 'mug shot' taken, hung on the wall – which is actually a portion of the general store – and then is given a plate of Joy's homemade cream puffs!

That's not all Joy does to make Little Cranberry, population 90, a friendlier place. She operates a mail-order stamp business that is so popular her tiny post office ranks fourth in sales out of 450 outlets in Maine. Why? Most of Joy's customers are summer visitors who want to stay in contact with the island. Joy sends a snapshot of an island scene and a hand-written note about island events along with each order.

One of the residents has said, 'She invents ways to bring pleasure to others.' Joy has received praise from the US Postmaster General and has the warm affection not only of the local residents but friends across America who delight in corresponding with her.

Why not ask the Lord to give you creative ideas which will brighten someone's life today. Perhaps a brief telephone call or postcard will remind them how important they really are to you and to God, their Heavenly Father.

Kind words can be short
and easy to speak,
but their echoes are
truly endless

She opens her mouth with skilful and
godly Wisdom, and in her tongue is the
law of kindness – giving counsel and
instruction.
Proverbs 31:26 AMP

Many years ago a famous singer was contracted to perform at a Paris opera house. The event was sold out in a matter of days. The entire city was abuzz with anticipation. That night the hall was packed with smartly-dressed men and women eager to hear the much-admired musician. The house manager took the stage and announced, 'Ladies and gentlemen, thank you for your enthusiastic support. I am afraid that due to illness, the woman whom you've all come to hear will not be performing tonight. However, we have found a suitable substitute we hope will provide you with comparable entertainment.'

The crowd groaned so loudly in its disappointment that few heard the singer's name. Frustration replaced excitement in the hall. The stand-in singer gave everything she had, but when her performance was over she was met with an uncomfortable silence rather than applause. Then, from the balcony, a child stood up and shouted, 'Mummy, I think you are wonderful!'

The crowd immediately responded with a thunderous ovation.

Once in a while we each need to hear somebody say, 'I think you are wonderful.' Why not be the person who gives that kind word of encouragement today!

Nothing beats
love at first sight except
live with insight

The beginning of wisdom is this:
Get wisdom, and whatever else you get,
get insight.
Proverbs 4:7 NRSV

Two lifelong friends in their early 50s began to argue over the forthcoming marriage of one of them to a man who was only in his 30s.

'I just don't believe in May-December marriages,' the friend said. 'After all, December is going to find in May the strength and virility of springtime, but whatever is May going to find in December?'

The bride-to-be thought for a moment and then replied with a twinkle in her eye, 'Christmas.'

Many couples who claim they 'fell in love at first sight' look back after years of marriage and adjust their opinions, saying, 'I was infatuated', or 'We felt an immediate attraction', or 'There was electricity between us when we first met'. Love, however, is a word they have come to cherish – it is something they now share that is far richer and more meaningful than the emotions they felt 'at first sight'.

One of the great qualities about genuine love is that it grows and deepens over time. Time is life's nursery for love. Tend to it as you would your most cherished plant and love's fragrance will continually remain.

A house is made of
walls and beams;
a home is made of
love and dreams

*Better a meal of vegetables where there is
love than a fattened calf with hatred*
Proverbs 15:17 NIV

In *Little House in the Ozarks*,[6] Laura Ingalls Wilder writes, 'I spent an afternoon a short time ago with a friend in her new home. The house was beautiful and well-furnished with new furniture, but it seemed bare and empty to me. I wondered why this was until I remembered my experience with my new house. I could not make the living room seem homelike. I would move the chairs here and there and change the pictures on the wall, but something was lacking. Nothing seemed to change the feeling of coldness and vacancy that displeased me whenever I entered the room.

'Then, as I stood in the middle of the room one day wondering what I could possibly do to improve it, it came to me that all that was needed was for someone to live in it and furnish it with everyday, pleasant thoughts of friendship and cheerfulness and hospitality.'

A homely atmosphere is not a matter of the right decorations; it emanates from the thoughts and feelings of the people who live there. Feelings of warmth and welcome can be created only by people who are kind, generous and even tempered. Why not determine to 'warm-up' the atmosphere where you live today?

The best way to hold a man is in your arms

The man should give his wife all that is
her right as a married woman,
and the wife should do the same
for her husband.
1 Corinthians 7:3 TLB

This old childhood rhyme is one that many people remember:

> Kiss and hug,
> Kiss and hug,
> Kiss your sweety
> On the mug.

While the rhyme was one children would use in ridiculing the puppy-love behaviour of their older brothers and sisters, the practice of kissing and hugging actually has many healthful benefits beyond those of building a loving relationship.

A West German magazine reported the results of a study conducted by a life insurance company. The researchers discovered that husbands who kiss their wives every morning:

- live an average of five years longer,
- are involved in fewer automobile accidents,
- are ill 50 per cent less, as noted by sick days, and
- earn 20 to 30 per cent more money.

Other researchers have found that kissing and hugging releases endorphins, giving mind and body a sense of genuine well-being that is translated into better health.

A kiss a day just may keep the doctor away!

Ninety per cent of the
friction of daily life is
caused by the
wrong tone of voice

A man finds joy in giving an apt reply –
and how good is a timely word!
Proverbs 15:23 NIV

A demanding wife continually nagged her husband to conform to her very high standards: 'This is how you should act, this is how you should dress, this is what you should say, this is where you should be seen, and this is how you should plan your career!' She insisted every aspect of his life be honed to perfection. Feeling thoroughly whipped, the man finally said, 'Why don't you just write it all down? Then you won't have to tell me these things all the time.' She gladly complied.

A short time later the wife died. Within the course of a year, the man met another woman and married. His new life seemed to be a perpetual honeymoon. He could hardly believe the great joy, and relief he was experiencing with his new bride.

One day he came across the list of 'do's and don'ts' his first wife had written. He read them and realised, to his amazement, he was following all of the instructions – even though his second wife had never mentioned them.

He thought about what might have happened and finally said to a friend, 'My former wife began her statements, "I hate it when . . ." but my new wife says, "I just love it when . . ."

Forgiveness is giving love when there is no reason to . . .

Blessed are the merciful, for they shall obtain mercy.

Matthew 5:7 NKJ

Lisa was shocked when she discovered that David had run up thousands of dollars on every one of their credit cards. Not only was she furious about the mountain of debt, she was frustrated with herself for not recognising David's habit of compulsive spending.

In the days that followed she wondered if she could ever trust her husband again, and whether they would ever be able to get out of debt.

Rather than wait for something to happen, she took two bold steps. The first was to convince David he needed help, and the second was to seek out a financial planner. She learned if she carefully monitored the family funds, they could be out of debt in a few years. This brought hope for her financial future and for the future of their marriage.

Another turnaround in their marriage came when David asked Lisa to forgive him. She found that forgiving David freed her to turn away from the matter of money and to focus on their relationship. She decided it was possible to love someone even though they had 'messed up'. Forgiving made trust possible again, and once trust was re-established their marriage began to be healed.

Forgiveness turns the heart away from what was and is, to what can be. Is it time for you to take some bold steps? If love is your motive, be encouraged! Situations can change.

Nothing is so strong
as gentleness.
Nothing is so gentle
as real strength.

You have given me your salvation as my
shield. Your right hand, O Lord, supports
me; your gentleness has made me great.
Psalm 18:35 TLB

Mentor Graham was so absorbed in evaluating assignments he failed to notice the youthful giant who slouched into his Illinois schoolroom one day after school. After his eyes had adjusted to the brightness of the late-afternoon sunshine, causing the husky young man to be in silhouette before him, he recognised the youth as a newcomer to the community. The lad already had a reputation for 'whipping the daylights' out of all the local toughs.

Graham would have been justified in thinking, What does he want here? Am I in danger? Rather, he looked up and down the six-foot-four-inches of muscle and ignorance before him and offered to help the lad with his reading. When the young man left the schoolroom an hour later, he had several books under his arm – a loan from Mentor Graham with a promise of more in the future.

Few people remember Graham. He was a quiet man, simply willing to do his best for any student who came his way. His pupil, however, became far more famous. His name was Abraham Lincoln.

A kind, helpful response to others is often perceived by them as strength. It is this gentle strength to which we are drawn. When you think you find yourself in a touchy situation, try a gentle touch!

Everyone has patience. Successful people learn to use it.

But let patience have its perfect work, that you may be perfect and complete, lacking nothing.

James 1:4 NKJ

Several years ago the driver of a speedboat was in a serious accident. In recounting what had happened, she said that she had been going at top speed when her boat veered just slightly, hitting a wave at a dangerous angle. The combined force of her speed and the size and angle of the wave sent the boat spinning wildly into the air. She was thrown from her seat and propelled deeply into the water. She was thrust so deep that she could not see any light from the surface. Being a little dazed, she had no idea which direction was 'up'.

Rather than panic, the woman remained calm and waited for the buoyancy of her life jacket to begin pulling her up. Then she swam heartily in that direction.

We often find ourselves surrounded by many voices, each with a different opinion, and we simply don't know which way is 'up'. When this happens we need to exercise patience and spend time with the Lord. We must read His Word, the Bible. And wait for His gentle tug on our hearts to pull us towards His will. The more we read, the more confident we will become, especially when His written Word and that gentle tug on our hearts come into agreement.

Remember, a few minutes, hours, days or even months of 'waiting' may mean the difference between sinking or floating!

Watch out for
temptation –
the more you see of it
the better it looks.

Keep watch, and pray
that you will not fall into temptation.
Mark 14:38 GNB

As a teen, Megan arrived home from school just in time to watch an hour of 'soap operas' before doing her homework. She enjoyed the escape into the TV world and wasn't really aware that the programmes were creating an inordinate amount of sexual curiosity in her. Over months and even years of watching her two 'soaps', Megan's perspective on life took a shift. She began to think, *Relationships don't need to be pure – in fact, the impure ones seem more exciting. Fidelity doesn't matter, as long as a person is 'happy'.*

As a college student, Megan found it easy to participate in 'one-night stands'. Then, after a short marriage ended in catastrophe as a result of her infidelity, she sought help from a counsellor. At the outset, it was difficult for the counsellor to understand why Megan had engaged in extramarital affairs. She had been a model teenager at home, church and school as far as her 'public' behaviour was concerned. Finally, the counsellor discovered the source of the temptation that drove Megan to participate in her supposed 'hidden' life.

What we see on TV inevitably becomes a part of our memory bank, becoming background information for 'justified' behaviour. If what you see isn't what you want to do, then change what you see!

It is such a comfort
to drop
the tangles of life
into God's hands
and leave them there.

Cast your cares on the LORD
and he will sustain you.
Psalm 55:22 NIV

Many years ago, a young woman who felt called to the ministry was accepted into a noted seminary. There were only two other women enrolled, and her very presence seemed to make her male classmates uncomfortable. She felt isolated yet on display at the same time. To make matters worse, many of her professors were doing their best to destroy her faith rather than build it up. Even her private time of devotions seemed dry and lonely.

At the Christmas break, she sought her father's counsel: 'How can I be strong in my resolve and straight in my theology with all that I face there?'

Her father took a pencil from his pocket and laid it on the palm of his hand. 'Can that pencil stand upright by itself?' he asked her.

'No,' she replied. Then her father grasped the pencil in his hand and held it in an upright position. 'Ah,' she said, 'but you are holding it now.'

'Daughter,' he replied, 'your life is like this pencil. But Jesus Christ is the one who can hold you.' The young woman took her pencil and returned to seminary.

Friendship
improves happiness,
and abates misery,
by doubling our joy,
and dividing our grief.

A friend loves at all times,
and a brother is born for adversity.
Proverbs 17:17 NIV

They call themselves the 'Ladies of the Lake', but they never set out to be a club. Rather, the group began when one of the women returned home exhausted from a business trip and came to the conclusion that she had too much of one thing in her life: MEN! With a husband and two boys at home, a work environment that was mostly male, and an elderly father and uncle for which to care, she resolved to set some time aside for herself and a few female friends.

Over the years, Paula hadn't cultivated very many friendships with other women, but she was determined to see that change. Eventually she discovered three like-minded women: one owned a machine shop, one worked for a contractor and one ran a transport café. The women pulled out their calendars over dinner one evening and agreed on this schedule – 'A trip to the lake at least once a quarter!'

At the lake, the women would listen to Mozart, fix gourmet dinners and sit on the deck overlooking the water. They would talk for hours – about everything – without an agenda.

Over the years, they became very close and often refer to each others as 'sisters'. Says Paula, 'Nobody understands like another woman.'

Everyone has an
invisible sign
hanging from his
neck saying,
'Make me feel
important!'

Therefore encourage one another
and build each other up,
just as in fact you are doing.
1 Thessalonians 5:11 NIV

It Isn't Enough

It isn't enough to say in our hearts
That we like a man for his ways,
It isn't enough that we fill our minds
With paeans of silent praise;
Nor is it enough that we honour a man
As our confidence upward mounts,
It's going right up to the man himself,
And telling him so that counts!
If a man does a work you really admire,
Don't leave a kind word unsaid.
In fear that to do so might make him vain
And cause him to 'lose his head'.
But reach out your hand and tell him,
'Well done', and see how his gratitude swells'
It isn't the flowers we strew on the grave,
It's the word to the living that tells.

Anonymous

For lack of praise, many think others draw negative conclusions about them. We can actually wound people by withholding our praise. Let someone know you think well of him or her today. What a difference your words will make!

You cannot do a
kindness too soon,
because you never
know how soon
it will be too late!

But encourage one another day after day,
as long as it is still called 'Today'.
Hebrews 3:13 NASB

William McKinley served in Congress before he was elected the 25th President of the United States. On his way to his congressional office one morning, he boarded a streetcar and took the only remaining seat. Minutes later, a woman who appeared to be ill boarded the car. Unable to find a seat, she clutched an overhead strap next to one of McKinley's colleagues. The other congressman hid behind his newspaper and did not offer the woman his seat. McKinley walked up the aisle, tapped the woman on the shoulder, offered her his seat and took her place in the aisle.

Years later when McKinley was President, this same congressman was recommended to him for a post as ambassador to a foreign nation. McKinley refused to appoint him. He feared a man who didn't have the courtesy to offer his seat to a sick woman in a crowded streetcar would lack the courtesy and sensitivity necessary to be an ambassador in a troubled nation. The disappointed congressman bemoaned his fate to many in Washington, but never did learn why McKinley chose someone else for the position.

Acts of kindness can lead you to prominence. Then, from that position of prominence, you can be kind to even more people!

Stack every bit of criticism between two layers of praise.

Correct, rebuke and encourage – with great patience and careful instruction

2 Timothy 4:2 NIV

Shortly after graduation, Joe and Lana married. One of their first marital discoveries was their very different understanding of 'being on time'. Not wanting to end the honeymoon stage too early, Lana found herself mildly complaining about Joe's being late. But Joe never took the hint, and soon her complaining turned to outright criticism.

On the surface, there may not seem to be much difference between exposing a problem and criticising it, but in a relationship, the choice of words can bring very different responses. Criticism attacks someone's personality and character. When Lana *criticised* Joe, she would say, 'You're only thinking about yourself!'

Putting an issue on the table for discussion in a positive manner is the first step towards finding a resolution. A person who asks gently, 'Does it embarrass you when we are late?' is opening a dialogue for finding the solution to the problem. Criticism only wounds the spirit, puts the other person on the defensive and usually ends up in a no-resolution argument.

Watch what you say! Criticism can cause a wound that takes years to heal, but a kind and gracious attitude in problem-solving can save you years of tears!

In trying times,
don't quit trying.

And let us not grow weary in well-doing,
for in due season we shall reap,
if we do not lose heart.

Galatians 6:9 RSV

Somebody said that it couldn't be done,
But he with a chuckle replied,
That 'maybe it couldn't' but he would be one
Who wouldn't say so till he'd tried.
So he buckled right in with the trace of a grin
On his face. If he worried, he hid it.
He started to sing as he tackled the thing
That couldn't be done. And he did it.
Somebody scoffed: 'Oh, you'll never do that,
At least no one ever has done it.'
But he took off his coat and he took off his hat
And the first thing he knew he'd begun it.
With the lift of his chin and a bit of a grin,
If any doubt rose he forbid it;
He started to sing as he tackled the thing
That couldn't be done, and he did it.
There are thousands to tell you it cannot be done,
There are thousands to prophesy failure;
There are thousands to point out to you, one by one,
The dangers that wait to assail you.
But just buckle right in with a bit of a grin,
Then take off your coat and go to it.
Just start in to sing as you tackle the thing
That cannot be done, and you'll do it.

Unknown

To love what you do
and feel that it matters –
how could anything be
more fun?

When you eat the labour of your hands,
you shall be happy,
and it shall be well with you.
Psalm 128:2 NKJ

A newspaper in England once asked this question of its readers, 'Who are the happiest people on the earth?'

The four prize-winning answers were:
• A little child building sand castles.
• A craftsman or artist whistling over a job well done.
• A mother, bathing her baby after a busy day.
• A doctor who has finished a difficult and dangerous operation that saved a human life.

The paper's editors were surprised to find virtually no one submitted kings, emperors, millionaires or others of riches and rank as the happiest people on earth.

W. Beran Wolfe once said, 'If you observe a really happy man you will find him building a boat, writing a symphony, educating his son, growing double dahlias in his garden or looking for dinosaur eggs in the Gobi Desert. He will not be searching for happiness as if it were a collar button that has rolled under the radiator. He will not be striving for it as a goal in itself. He will have become aware that he is happy in the course of living life twenty-four crowded hours of the day.'

Life is a coin.
You can spend it
anyway you wish,
but you can only
spend it once.

*For what is your life? It
is even a vapour that appears
for a little time and then vanishes away.*
James 4:14 NKJ

Anita Septimus has worked as a social worker for HIV-infected children since 1985. In the first few months she worked with her tiny clients, three of them died. Despair began to overwhelm her. She made a commitment to stick with the job for three more months, during which time she could not get a friend's words out of her mind, 'You have not chosen a pretty profession'.

She had to admit, her friend was right. It took resolve to accept that fact and simply do what she could to help families make the most of what remained of their children's lives. She is still there.

Over the last ten years, her clinic has grown considerably. Today, Anita and her staff care for more than 300 families with AIDS children. They go into their homes, teach infection preventions and help the parents plan for the future. The children are regularly taken on trips to the zoo, the circus and summer camps.

One AIDS baby wasn't expected to see her first birthday, but she recently celebrated her tenth. Such 'long-term' clients give back to Anita what she terms 'an indestructible sense of hope' – a precious gift!

Diligence is the mother of good fortune.

The hand of the diligent
makes one rich.
Proverbs 10:4 NKJ

On a shelf sits a beautiful and expensive carving from the Orient. It is a statue of a lady wearing a tall headdress, and balanced atop the headdress is an intricately carved ball. Inside that seamless sphere is another slightly smaller sphere of equal intricacy – and inside that still another, and then another – until one can no longer see through the tiny carved holes to see how many more balls there actually are.

Several things make this orb truly remarkable. Each of the nested balls is seamless, completely free from the other outside it and inside it, and magnificent in its airy, lacy design. The orb was carved from a single piece of ivory over 100 years ago, before the days of electronic magnifying instruments.

Why did the artist carve so many layers with such precision? The smallest orb would not be clearly seen by most people, yet each one was finished with as much skill and artistry as was applied to the larger, outer ones.

The small details of a job may not always remain unnoticed or unseen. Like this artist, your excellence in small things can bring you blessing in this life and make you a legend for future generations to follow.

The most wasted
of all days
is that on which
one has not laughed.

A happy heart makes the face cheerful,
but heartache crushes the spirit.
Proverbs 15:13 NIV

A little girl was eating her breakfast one morning when a ray of sunlight suddenly appeared through the clouds and reflected off the spoon in her cereal bowl. She immediately put it into her mouth. With a big smile she exclaimed to her mother, 'I just swallowed a spoonful of sunshine!'

A spoonful of sunshine just may be the best 'soul food' that a person can have in a day. A prominent surgeon once wrote, 'Encourage your child to be merry and to laugh aloud. A good, hearty laugh expands the chest and makes the blood bound merrily along. A good laugh will sound right through the house. It will not only do your child good, but will be a benefit to all who hear, and be an important means of driving the blues away from a dwelling. Merriment is very catching, and spreads in a remarkable manner, few being able to resist the contagion. A hearty laugh is delightful harmony; indeed it is the best of music.'[7]

An old poem advises: If you are on the Gloomy Line, the Worry Train or the Grouchy Track, get a transfer! It's time to climb aboard the Sunshine Train and sit in one of its Cheerful cars.

You can accomplish more
in one hour with God
than one lifetime
without Him.

Walk in wisdom . . . redeeming the time.
Colossians 4:5 AV

In *A Closer Walk*,[8] Catherine Marshall writes about a neighbour, 'Cynthia felt she was losing her identity in an endless procession of social events and chauffeuring of children. During one cocktail party, Cynthia decided to limit herself to ginger ale and made some discoveries – not especially pleasant: "I saw our crowd through new eyes," she told me. "No one was really saying anything . . . All at once I began to ask questions about what we call 'the good life'."

'In a search for answers, Cynthia set aside an hour each day for meditation. As she did this over a period of weeks there came to her the realization that she was being met in this quiet hour by something more than her own thoughts and psyche . . . By Someone who loved her and insisted this love be passed on to her family and friends.'

Cynthia made changes in her life as the result of her 'hour with God'. She turned meal times into a time for family sharing. Family Game Night became a substitute for television once a week. She and her husband joined a Bible study that met twice a month. In all, Cynthia concluded, 'God . . . the Author of creativity, is ready to make a dull life adventuresome the moment we allow His Holy Spirit to go to work.'

Courage is
resistance to fear,
mastery of fear.
Not the absence of fear.

*Therefore, take up the full armour of God,
that you may be able to resist in the evil
day, and having done everything, to stand
firm. Stand firm therefore.*
Ephesians 6:13,14 NASB

Napoleon called Marshall Ney the bravest man he had ever known. Yet Ney's knees trembled so badly one morning before a battle, he had difficulty mounting his horse. When he finally was in the saddle, he shouted contemptuously down at his limbs, 'Shake away, knees. You would shake worse than that if you knew where I am going to take you.'

Courage is not a matter of not being afraid. It is a matter of taking action even when you are afraid!

Courage is also more than sheer bravado – shouting, 'I can do this!' and launching out with a do-or-die attitude over some reckless dare.

True courage is manifest when a person chooses to take a difficult or even dangerous course of action because it is the right thing to do. Courage is looking beyond yourself to what is best for another.

The source of all courage is the Holy Spirit of God, our Comforter. It is His nature to remain at our side to help us. When we welcome Him into our lives and He compels us to do something, we can confidently trust He will be right there, helping us get it done!

The art of being wise
is the art of knowing
what to overlook.

A man's wisdom gives him patience;
it is to his glory to overlook an offence.
Proverbs 19:11 NIV

The story is told of a couple at their golden wedding anniversary celebration. Surrounded by her children, grandchildren and great-grandchildren, the wife was asked the secret to a long and happy marriage. With a loving glance towards her husband, she answered: 'On my wedding day, I decided to make a list of ten of my husband's faults which, for the sake of our marriage, I would overlook. I figured I could live with at least ten faults.'

A guest asked her to identify some of the faults she had chosen to overlook. Her husband looked a bit troubled at the thought of having his foibles and flaws revealed to the assembled group. However, his wife sweetly replied, 'To tell you the truth, dear, I never did get around to listing them. Instead, everytime my husband did something that made me hopping mad, I would simply say to myself, *Lucky for him that's one of the ten!*'

Even the most devoted friends and spouses will experience storms in their relationships from time to time. Some problems are worth addressing in order to resolve them. Others are best left undiscussed. In time, issues of little importance tend to blow past without any need for a 'blow-up'.

Triumph is just 'umph' added to try.

And let us not get tired of doing what is right, for after a while we will reap a harvest of blessing if we don't get discouraged and give up.

Galatians 6:9 TLB

Monica Seles recently won her first tennis tournament in more than two years since she had been stabbed in the shoulder by a fanatical fan.

Withstanding 100° heat and tendinitis in her left knee, she roared through the Canadian Open to defeat three Top 20 players en route to a finals match that lasted only 51 minutes. Her nightmare recovery had truly come to an end.

To help in her recovery, Monica asked Olympic champion Jackie Joyner-Kersee and her coach/husband Bob Kersee, to put her on a strict workout routine. While on this physical regimen she also worked to overcome the emotional problems that accompany such an attack.

Her father and coach, Karolj, who had been stricken by prostate and stomach cancer, was her continual source of inspiration. She said. 'I was down and he came into my room and said he couldn't stand to see me that way. I decided then that I had to try and put it behind me and move on.'

Have you ever felt 'stabbed in the back' while doing good? Withdrawal is often our first temptation, but with a creative and loving God, who continually inspires us, we just can't quit! Our detractors will have to say about us what was said about Monica, 'She's back!'

People don't care how
much you know,
until they know
how much you care . . .
about them.

*And though I have the gift of prophecy,
and understand all mysteries and all
knowledge, and though I have all faith, so
that I could remove mountains, but have
not love, I am nothing.*
1 Corinthians 13:2 NKJ

On a bitter cold Virginia evening, an old man waited on a path by a river, hoping for someone on a horse to carry him across. His beard was glazed with frost and his body grew numb before he finally heard the thunder of horses' hooves. Anxiously he watched as several horsemen appeared. He let the first pass by without making an effort to get his attention, then another and another. Finally, only one rider remained. As he drew near, the old man caught his eye and asked 'Sir, would you mind giving me a ride to the other side?'

The rider helped the man onto his horse and, sensing he was half-frozen, decided to take him all the way home, which was several miles out of the way. As they rode, the horseman asked. 'Why didn't you ask one of the other men to help you? I was the last one. What if I had refused?' The old man said, 'I've been around a while, son, and I know people pretty well. When I looked into their eyes and saw they had no concern for my condition, I knew it was useless to ask. When I looked into your eyes, I saw kindness and compassion.'

At the door of the old man's house the rider resolved, 'May I never get too busy in my own affairs that I fail to respond to the needs of others.' And with that, Thomas Jefferson turned and directed his horse back to the White House.

Good words are worth much, and cost little

Pleasant words are a honeycomb, sweet to the soul and healing to the bones.

Proverbs 16:24 NIV

It takes the same amount of energy to say a positive word as it does a negative one. In fact, it may take even less. Research has shown that when we speak positive words – even in difficult circumstances or troubling situations – our bodies relax. As we relax, blood flow increases, including the flow of blood to the brain. A well-oxygenated brain is much more likely to think creatively, make wise decisions, find reasonable solutions and generate answers to questions.

Positive words ease relationships and create an atmosphere of peace that is conducive to rest, relaxation, rejuvenation and sleep – all of which are necessary for good health.

On the other hand, contrary to popular thought, negative words do not release tension . . . they keep the body in a state of tension, constricting muscles and blood vessels. Irrational, uncreative, unreasonable behaviour is a secondary effect.

A continual flow of negative words causes relationships to suffer, which creates an atmosphere of disharmony and makes for fitful sleep and frayed nerves – none of which are healthy!

One of the best things we can do for our overall health is to transform our speech habits!

I don't know
the secret to success
but the key to failure
is to try to please
everyone

No one can serve two masters;
for either he will hate the one and love the
other, or he will hold to one
and despise the other.
Matthew 6:24 NASB

The story is told of a painter who desired to produce one work which would please the entire world. She drew a picture which required her utmost skill and took it to the marketplace. She posted directions at the bottom of the piece for spectators to mark with a brush each portion of the picture that didn't meet their approval. The spectators came and, in general, applauded the work. But each, eager to make a personal critique, marked a small portion of the picture. By evening, the painter was mortified to find the entire picture had become a blot.

The next day the painter returned with a copy of the first picture. This time she asked the spectators to mark the portions of the work they admired. The spectators again complied. When the artist returned several hours later, she found every stroke that had been panned the day before had received praise by this day's critics.

The artist concluded, 'I now believe the best way to please half of the world is not to mind what the other half says.'

People will always have an opinion about what we say or do. That is why we live our lives according to the words of the Bible – God's opinion. Then we will not fret over the opinions of others.

No one is useless in
this world
who lightens the burden
of it to anyone else.

Bear one another's burdens,
and so fulfil the law of Christ.
Galatians 6:2 RSV

Carol Porter, a registered nurse, is a co-founder of Kid-Care, Inc., a non-profit-making group with a volunteer staff who deliver 500 free meals each day to poor neighbourhoods. Each meal is prepared in Porter's cramped Houston home, where extra stoves and refrigerators have been installed in what used to be the family's living room and den. Kid-Care receives no public funding, and although Carol's efforts have resulted in help from some corporations, most of her $500,000 budget comes from individual donations.

Carol credits her late mother, Lula Doe, for giving her the idea for Kid-Care. In 1984, Lula persuaded a local supermarket not to discard its blemished produce, but to let her distribute it to the poor.

During Christmastime in 1989, Carol saw a group of children searching for food in a McDonald's dumpster. She says, 'I saw Third World conditions a stone's throw from where I live.' Kid-Care was her response.

'People ask me what's in it for me. And I tell them to go the route with me and see my kids' faces. That's what's in it for me.' She sees the meals as 'better than ice cream . . . It's hope'.[8]

Purpose in life comes when we purpose to lift the load of another . . . to show God's love by doing for them what they could not do for themselves!

Do not follow where
the path may lead –
go instead where
there is no path
and leave a trail.

Your ears shall hear a word behind you,
saying, 'This is the way, walk in it'.
Isaiah 30:21 NKJ

Many years ago, an intern in a New York hospital heard a surgeon bemoan the fact that most brain tumours were fatal. The surgeon predicted some day a surgeon would discover how to save the lives of these patients. Intern Ernest Sachs dared to be that surgeon. At the time, the leading expert on the anatomy of the brain was Sir Victor Horsley. Sachs received permission to study under him, but felt he should prepare for the experience by studying for six months under some of the most able physicians in Germany. Then he went to England, where for two years he assisted Dr Horsley in doing long and intricate experiments on dozens of monkeys.

When Sachs returned to America he was ridiculed for requesting the opportunity to treat brain tumours. For years he fought obstacles and discouragement, driven by an uncontrollable urge to succeed in his quest. Today, largely thanks to Dr Sachs, the majority of brain tumours can be cured. His book, *The Diagnosis and Treatment of Brain Tumors*, is considered the standard authority on the subject.

Beause something *isn't* being done presently doesn't mean it *can't* be done. And maybe you are the one to do it!

There is one thing alone
that stands the brunt of life
throughout its length;
a quiet conscience.

If our hearts do not condemn us,
we have confidence before God.
1 John 3:21 NIV

President Woodrow Wilson was approached one day by one of his secretaries, who suggested he take time off from his work to enjoy a particular diversion he enjoyed. President Wilson replied, 'My boss won't let me do it.'

'Your boss?' the secretary asked, wondering who could be the boss of the chief executive of the United States.

'Yes,' said Wilson. 'I have a conscience that is my boss. It drives me to the task, and will not let me accept this tempting invitation.'

Our conscience is one of the most prized items we possess. It is through our conscience that we receive inner promptings from God which, when in agreement with our actions, will point us towards a safe and eternal way.

It has been said, 'A conscience is like a thermostat on an air conditioning unit – it kicks in when things are on the verge of getting too hot.'

It is possible to ignore our conscience and 'follow the crowd,' but this is a sad waste of our lives. The conscience is the window to the soul through which we hear the voice of God, who always leads us to succes and inner peace.

Listen carefully, He may have something good to say!

My obligation is to do
the right thing.
The rest is in God's hands.

*If you know that he is righteous,
you may be sure that every one who
does right is born of him.*
1 John 2:29 RSV

In *Dakota*,[9] Kathleen Norris writes: 'A Benedictine sister from the Philippines once told me what her community did when some sisters took to the streets in the popular revolt against the Marcos regime. Some did not think it proper for nuns to demonstrate in public, let alone risk arrest. In a group meeting that began and ended with prayer, the sisters who wished to continue demonstrating explained that this was for them a religious obligation; those who disapproved also had their say. Everyone spoke; everyone heard and gave counsel.

'It was eventually decided that the nuns who were demonstrating should continue to do so; those who wished to expres solidarity but were unable to march would prepare food and provide medical assistance to the demonstrators, and those who disapproved would pray for everyone. The sisters laughed and said, "If one of the conservative sisters was praying that we young, crazy ones would come to our senses and stay off the streets, that was O.K. We were still a community." '[9]

God calls some to action, others to support and still others to pray. Each will be doing what is 'right' in His eyes if they obey His call!

Expect great things
from God.
Attempt great things
for God.

*Truly, truly, I say to you, he who believes
in Me, the works that I do shall he do also;
and greater works than these shall he do;
because I go to the Father.*
John 14:12 NASB

Gladys Aylward saw herself as a simple woman who just did what God called her to do. Yet, her life was so remarkable that both a book (*The Small Woman*) and a film (*The Inn of the Sixth Happiness*) were produced about the great things God accomplished through her.

A British citizen, Aylward left her home in 1920 and sailed for China. There she bought orphans who were being systematically discarded, children who had been displaced by the political upheavals of the time and left to starve or wander on their own until placed in government warehouses. Gladys gave these children a home.

When the Japanese invaded China, she was forced to flee the mainland with 100 children. She ended up on the island of Formosa with her charges. There she continued to devote her life to raising children who knew no other mother.

Gladys explained her amazing work for God like this: 'I did not choose this. I was led into it by God. I am not really more interested in children than I am in other people, but God through His Holy Spirit gave me to understand that this is what He wanted me to do, so I did.'

Doest thou love life? Then
do not
squander time,
for that is the stuff
life is made of.

Remember how short my time is.
Psalm 89:47 AV

A woman once had a dream that an angel was giving her this message: 'As a reward for your virtues, the sum of $1,440 will be deposited into your bank account every morning. This amount has only one condition. At the close of each business day, any balance that has not been used will be cancelled. It won't carry over to the next day or accrue interest. Each morning, a new $1,440 will be credited to you.'

The dream was so vivid, she asked the Lord to show her what it meant. He led her to realise she was receiving 1,440 minutes every morning, the total number of minutes in a twenty-four-hour day What she did with this deposit of time was important, because 1,440 minutes per day was all she would ever receive.

Each of us has a similar account. At the close of each 'business' day, we should be able to look over our ledger and see that these golden minutes were spent wisely.

Time is God's gift to you. What you do with your time is your gift to God.

The grass may be
greener on the
other side,
but it still has to
be mowed.

Be content with such things as you have.
Hebrews 13:5 NKJ

Several years ago, a newspaper cartoon was drawn of two fields divided by a fence. Both were about the same size and each had plenty of lush green grass.

Each field had a mule whose head stuck through the wire fence, eating grass from the other's pasture. Although each mule was surrounded by plenty of grass, the neighbouring field seemed somewhat more desirable – even though it was harder to reach.

In the process, the mules' heads became caught in the fence. They panicked and brayed uncontrollably at being unable to free themselves. The cartoonist wisely described the situation with one caption: 'DISCONTENT'.

Like the mules, when we focus on what we don't have we become blinded to the blessings which surround us. There is nothing wrong with desiring something, but to think life is easier in someone else's pasture may not be true. Besides, no matter whose pasture we are in, we will always have to deal with the attitudes of our own heart.

If there is something you desire in life, perhaps a home, a better car or even your own business, look to Jesus to help you bring it to pass. And while He is working on it, remember to find pleasure in what He's already given you!

Every job is a
self-portrait
of the person who does it.
Autograph your work
with excellence.

'Many daughters have done well, but you excel them all.'

Proverbs 31:29 NKJ

Someone once asked Al Jolson, a popular musical comedy star of the twenties, what he did to warm up a cold audience. Jolson answered, 'Whenever I go out before an audience and don't get the response I feel that I ought to get . . . I don't go back behind the scenes and say to myself, "That audience is dead from the neck up – it's a bunch of wooden nutmegs." No, instead I say to myself, "Look here, Al, what is wrong with you tonight? The audience is all right, but you're all wrong, Al."'

Many a performer has blamed a poor showing on an audience. Al Jolson took a different approach. He tried to give the best performance of his career to his coldest, most unresponsive audiences . . . and the result was that before an evening was over, he had them applauding and begging for more.

You'll always be able to find excuses for mediocrity. In fact, a person intent on justifying a bad performance usually has excuses lined up before the final curtain falls. Choose instead to put your full energy into your performance. Your extra effort will turn an average performance into something outstanding.

Ah! . . . the joys of a job well done . . . that is true satisfaction!

The greatest achievements are those that benefit others.

To be the greatest, be a servant.
Matthew 23:11 TLB

A recent plot of the American soap opera *All My Children* called for high-society philanthropist Brooke English to move into a homeless shelter to better understand their plight. Julia Barr, who plays Brooke, felt promoted by the part to take some real-life action of her own. She became a participant in First Step, a New York City job-readiness programme for homeless and formerly homeless women. The eight-week session included one-to-one counselling, advice on CVs, access to job apprenticeships, interview clothes, and pep talks for people such as herself.

Says Julia, 'I know how it feels to lack motivation and self-esteem. I tend to procrastinate, I'm rarely on time, I'm rather bossy, I'm very stubborn – we *all* have things that hold us back and so I share mine.'[10]

Julia is not only giving her time, but also her money. When her maternal grandmother, Myrtle, died at the age of 104, she left Julia 'a nice amount of money'. It was all donated to First Step.

Julia Barr has one Emmy award and six nominations, but those in First Step will remember her for the care she gave to them.

If a task is once
begun, never leave it
till it's done.
Be the labour great or small,
do it well or
not at all.

Whatever your hand finds to do,
do it with your might.
Ecclesiastes 9:10 NKJ

A series of illustrations in a popular magazine once depicted the life-story of a 'one-note musician'. From frame to frame, the tale revealed how the woman followed her daily routine of eating and sleeping until the time came for the evening concert. She carefully inspected her violin, took her seat among the other violinists, arranged her music on the stand and tuned her instrument. As the concert began, the conductor skillfully cued first one group of musicians and then another until finally, the crucial moment arrived. It was time for the one note to be played!

The conductor turned to the violinist and signalled her to sound her note. She did, and then the moment was over. The orchestra played on and the 'one-note' woman sat quietly through the rest of the concert – not with a sense of disappointment that she had played only one note, but with a sense of contentment and peace of mind that she had played her one note in tune, on time and with great gusto.

Sometimes 'one-note' people are criticised for being limited or narrow in their perspective by those whose lifestyle requires the wearing of many 'hats'. But a job well done by others is valued by God, so it certainly deserves our recognition and respect.

I would rather
walk with God
in the dark
than go alone
in the light.

Even when walking through the dark
valley of death I will not be afraid,
for you are close beside me,
guarding, guiding all the way.
Psalm 23:4 TLB

On February 11, 1861, President-elect Lincoln left his home in Springfield to begin his rail journey to Washington, where he was to be inaugurated a month later. Lincoln had a premonition this would be the last time he would see Springfield. Standing on the rear platform of his railroad car, he bid the townspeople farewell. He closed his remarks with these words: 'Today I leave you. I go to assume a task more difficult than that which devolved upon General Washington. The great God which guided him must help me. Without that assistance I shall surely fail; with it, I cannot fail.'

The same is true for us, regardless of the tasks we face. Without God's assistance, we cannot succeed. We may get the dishes washed, the laundry folded and the beds made . . . we may get our work done without accident or incident . . . we may find what we need at the market and manage to keep a schedule. But without God's help, our lives would be a confused mess.

Does God care about what happens in our day? Absolutely! When we become overwhelmed, making the smallest tasks into mountains, He helps us to 'gather ourselves'. Step-by-step He shows us the way and our strength is renewed to go on.

All our dreams can
come true –
if we have the
courage to
pursue them.

Be strong and courageous, and act;
do not fear nor be dismayed,
for the Lord God, my God, is with you.
1 Chronicles 28:20 NASB

Sports psychologists have identified six recurring traits common among gold-medalist athletes. These 'traits of a champion' apply to both men and women, and are also dominant factors in the lives of those who succeed in non-athletic vocations.

1. *Self-analysis.* The successful athlete knows her strengths and weaknesses, and engages in critical appraisal that is honest, but never negative.

2. *Self-competition.* A winner knows she can only control her own performance, so she competes against her own best effort, not that of others.

3. *Focus.* The champion is always 'in the present', concentrating on the task at hand.

4. *Confidence.* Successful athletes control anxiety by setting tough, but reasonable goals. As goals are reached, confidence increases.

5. *Toughness.* This is a mental trait that involves accepting risk and trying to win, rather than trying not to lose. A winner sees change as opportunity and accepts responsibility for her own destiny.

6. *Having a game plan.* Even elite athletes know talent is not enough. They have a game plan.[11]

Everyone can develop these traits. Everyone!

Remember the banana –
when it left the bunch,
it got skinned.

Let us not hold aloof from our church meetings, as some do. Let us do all we can to help one another's faith, and this the more earnestly as we see the final day drawing nearer.
Hebrews 10:25 JBP

The next time you visit a very dense forest, try to imagine what is taking place under your feet. Scientists now know that when the roots of trees come into contact with one another, a substance is released which encourages the growth of a particular kind of fungus. This fungus helps link roots of different trees – even those of dissimilar species. If one tree has access to water, another to nutrients, and a third to sunlight, the fungus enables the transfer of these items to trees that may be in need. Thus the trees have the means of sharing with one another to preserve them all.

Our culture today applauds individualism. This isolates people from one another and cuts them off from the mainstream of life. With more and more people working at home or in walled offices, and with schedules crammed tighter than ever with work and activities, feelings of loneliness are more likely to increase than decrease. Don't allow isolation to overcome you!

Reach out to others. Begin to give when you can. Learn to receive when others give to you. Build a network of friends, not just colleagues. And above all, root yourself into a group that nourishes you spiritually – a church.

Decisions can take you
out of God's will
but never out
of His reach

If we are faithless, he will remain faithful,
for he cannot disown himself.
2 Timothy 2:13 NIV

When Cathy met Jim at a badminton game, she thought he was the man for her – everything she was looking for! After several months of dating, Cathy was as sold on Jim as ever, except it bothered her that he found so many excuses for drinking alcohol. 'I got a raise!' 'My friend is getting married!' 'My sister is graduating from university!'

Despite her friends' warnings and her own misgivings, Cathy married Jim. Before long, however, the marriage was destroyed by his drinking. When the divorce was final, Cathy felt destroyed too. By ignoring the Holy Spirit's warnings and her friends' wise counsel, she had made one of the biggest mistakes a Christian could make. 'I wanted to have my way instead of God's,' Cathy told her pastor. 'I thought I knew what was best for me.'

'We all think that sometimes.' Cathy's pastor said. 'We forget that the One who created us knows us better than we know ourselves. But remember, Cathy, He never gives up on us! When we admit our mistakes, He always forgives us and gives us another chance.'

Recovering from the bad choices we've made can be heart-wrenching and difficult, but God is always right there, ready to make us whole and give us a brand new life.

'No' is one of the
few words
that can never be
misunderstood.

*'But let your statements be "Yes, yes"
or "No, no".'*
Matthew 5:37 NASB

While in medical training, surgeons are encouraged to weigh the importance of each word spoken during an operation. As the anaesthetic is given, fear may strike a patient if she hears someone say, 'I'm going to shoot her now'. Even a phrase such as 'Hook up the monitor' may be interpreted by a drugged patient as sounding like 'Shake up the monster'. Can you imagine the impact on a half-dazed patient if she hears a doctor say, 'This isn't my day!'

The same directions given by two different physicians could encourage or discourage a patient, simply by their tone of voice. One doctor's voice might suggest a prescription will work, while another's voice might convey reservations. Either would drastically affect the morale of a patient.

Theodore Roosevelt popularised an expression about the need for clear, precise communication. He called words with several possible meanings 'weasel words' – by using them a speaker might weasel out of any commitment, claiming a different interpretation of the word.

The Bible also tells us again and again to remember the importance of our words. We are to always speak words of encouragement, hope and faith to those around us.

Some people complain because God put thorns on roses, while others praise Him for putting roses among thorns.

Finally, brethren, whatsoever things are true, whatsoever things are honest, whatsoever things are just, whatsoever things are pure, whatsoever things are lovely, whatsoever things are of good report; if there be any virtue, and if there be any praise, think on these things.

Philippians 4:8 AV

One rainy day, a woman overheard someone say, 'What miserable weather!' She looked out of her office window to see a big fat robin using a nearby puddle of water for a bathtub. He was splashing and fluttering, thoroughly enjoying himself. She couldn't help but think, Miserable for whom? It's all a matter of perspective.'

That's a lesson that Lincoln Steffens learned as a young boy. He was watching an artist paint a picture of a muddy river. He told the artist he didn't like the picture because there was so much 'mud' in it. The artist admitted there was mud in the picture, but what he saw was the beautiful colours and contrasts of the light against the dark.

Steffens later preached in a sermon, 'Mud or beauty – which do we look for as we journey through life? If we look for mud and ugliness, we find them – they are there. Just as the artist found beauty in the muddy river, because that is what he was looking for, we will find, in the stream of life, those things which we desire to see. To look for the best and see the beautiful is the way to get the best out of life each day.'

Even the Bible says that what you see is what you get!

The bridge you burn now may be the one you later have to cross.

Do everything possible on your part to live in peace with everybody.

Romans 12:18 GNB

In *Learning to Forgive*, Doris Donnelly writes, 'Some years ago I met a family very proficient in the use of scissors . . . The friends of each family member were under constant scrutiny to determine whether they measured up to the standards imposed by mother and father. One slip . . . resulted in ostracism from the narrow circle of 'friends' . . . Anyone who did not respond immediately with profuse gratitude was eliminated from the list for the next time. Snip.

'Eventually I, too, was scissored out of their lives. I never knew for sure why, but I knew enough to recognise that once I was snipped away there was no hope of my being sewn into their lives again.

'Last year the mother of the family died. The father and daughters, expecting large crowds to gather to say their final farewells, enlisted the assistance of the local police to handle the traffic . . . Telegrams were sent . . . phone calls were made . . . local motels were alerted . . . yet in the end, only the husband, the daughters, their husbands and a grandchild or two attended the services.'[12]

Cutting imperfect people out of our lives is a prescription for loneliness. Who would remain to be our friends? Is there anyone you could sew back into your pattern? Why not give them a call?

Real friends are those who, when you've made a fool of yourself, don't feel you've done a permanent job.

Love . . . bears all things, believes all things, hopes all things, endures all things. Love never fails.
1 Corinthians 13:7,8 NKJ

Napoleon went to school in Brienne with a young man named Demasis who greatly admired him. After Napoleon quelled the mob in Paris and served at Toulon, his authority was stripped from him and he became penniless. We rarely think of Napoleon as struggling through hard times. However, with thoughts of suicide, he headed towards a bridge to throw himself into the waters below. On the way he met his old friend, Demasis, who asked him what was troubling him.

Napoleon told him bluntly he was without money, his mother was in need and he despaired of his situation ever changing. 'Oh, if that is all,' Demasis said, 'take this; it will supply your wants.' He put a pouch of gold into his hands and walked away. Normally, Napoleon would have never taken such a handout, but that night he did and his hope was renewed.

When Napoleon came to power, he sought far and wide to thank and promote his friend . . . but he never found him. It was rumoured that Demasis lived and served in one of Napoleon's own armies, but never revealed his true identity; rather, he was content to serve quietly in support of the leader he admired.

Sometimes our simple words or deeds make all the difference in the world to someone who doesn't know where to turn.

Most people wish to
serve God –
but only in an
advisory capacity.

*Humble yourselves therefore under the
mighty hand of God, that he may exalt
you in due time.*
1 Peter 5:6 AV

For weeks, eight-year-old Susie had been looking forward to a particular Saturday fishing trip with her dad. But when the day finally arrived, it was raining heavily.

Susie wandered around the house all morning, grumbling as she peered out of the windows, 'Seems like the Lord would know it would have been better to have the rain yesterday than today.' Her father tried to explain how important the rain was to the farmers and gardeners. But Susie only replied, 'It just isn't fair.'

Around three o'clock the rain stopped. There was still time for fishing, so father and daughter quickly loaded their gear and headed for the lake. Because of the rainstorm, the fish were really biting. Within a couple of hours, they returned with a full bucket of fish.

At the family's 'fish dinner' that night, Susie was asked to say grace. She concluded her prayer by saying, 'And, Lord, if I sounded grumpy early today, it was because I couldn't see far enough ahead.'

When we seek God's advice in our lives, it is important to realise He alone can see what's coming.

Conscience is God's built-in
warning system.
Be very happy
when it hurts you.
Be very worried
when it doesn't.

*So I always take pains to have a
clear conscience toward God
and toward men.*
Acts 24:16 RSV

Kelly was surprised to find a hairdryer tucked into a corner of an old suitcase. For years she had used the case to store bits of fabric from her sewing projects. Now, while piecing together a quilt, she had unearthed it. *Where did this come from?* she asked herself.

After several days of trying to remember, she recalled having used it while visiting a friend nearly a decade before. She had made several visits to the family and apparently had placed the borrowed hair dryer into her case inadvertently. To complicate matters, the family had asked about its whereabouts, and she had replied she didn't have a clue!

Embarrassed, she thought, *How can I tell my friends after all these years that I have this?* However, her conscience wouldn't let the matter rest. She finally sent the hairdryer back to the family with an apology and an explanation. With many laughs, all was quickly forgiven.

A healthy conscience is one of our greatest gifts from God. It serves to keep our lives on track and thus maintain peace in our hearts.

If you don't stand for something you'll fall for anything!

For ye are bought with a price: therefore glorify God in your body, and in your spirit, which are God's.

1 Corinthians 6:20 AV

A woman passed a particular corner each day on her way to work. For more than a week she observed a young girl trying to sell a floppy-eared puppy. The woman finally said to the girl, 'You know, if you really want to sell this dog, then I suggest you clean him up, brush his coat, raise your price and make people think they're getting something big.' At noon, the saleswoman noticed the girl had taken her advice. The puppy was groomed and sitting under a big sign: '*TREEMENNDOUS* Puppy for Sale – £2,000.'

The woman smiled and gulped, determined to tell the girl later that she might have overpriced the puppy. To her surprise, on the way home she saw the puppy had gone! Flabbergasted, the woman sought out the girl to ask if she had really sold the dog for £2,000.

The girl replied, 'I certainly did, and I want to thank you for all your help.' The woman stuttered, 'How in the world did you do it?' The girl said, 'It was easy. I just took two £1,000 cats in exchange!'

Two thousand years ago there was another great exchange. On a cross outside Jerusalem, Jesus Christ gave His life in exchange for ours. What value did He see in us? We were His prized creation, stolen for a season by our own will, but now repurchased as His beloved possession.

You should never let
adversity get you down –
except on your knees.

For I am persuaded, that neither death,
nor life, nor angels, nor principalities,
nor powers, nor things present,
nor things to come . . . shall be able
to separate us from the love of God,
which is in Christ Jesus our Lord.
Romans 8:38, 39 AV

Many people see abundant spring rains as a great blessing to farmers, especially if the rains come after the plants have sprouted and are several inches tall. What they don't realise is even a short drought can have a devastating effect on a crop of seedlings that have received too much rain.

Why? Because during frequent rains, the young plants are not required to push their roots deeper into the soil in search of water. If a drought occurs later, plants with shallow root systems will quickly die.

We often receive abundance into our lives – rich fellowship, great teaching, thorough 'soakings' of spiritual blessings. Yet, when stress or tragedy enters our lives, we may find ourselves thinking God has abandoned us or is unfaithful. The fact is, we have allowed the 'easiness' of our lives to keep us from pushing our spiritual roots deeper. We have allowed others to spoonfeed us, rather than develop our own deep personal relationship with God through prayer and study of His Word.

Only the deeply-rooted are able to endure hard times without wilting. The best advice is to enjoy the 'rain' while seeking to grow even closer to Him.

The best bridge
between hope
and despair
is often a good
night's sleep

It is vain for you to rise up early,
To sit up late,
To eat the bread of sorrows;
For so He gives His beloved sleep.
Psalm 127:2 NKJ

Medical researchers are coming to what may seem to be a commonsense conclusion: a missing ingredient to health may be 'vitamin Zzzzzzz.'

When participants in one study were cheated out of four hours of sleep for four consecutive nights, they had on average a 30 per cent drop in their immune systems, as measured by natural killer-cell activity. Such a drop can readily increase a person's susceptibility to colds and flu, and perhaps to other serious diseases. Says sleep researcher Michael Irwin, M.D., 'Many people just need a regular-length sleep to get those natural killer cells revved up again.'

While a steady diet of sufficient sleep may not completely prevent disease, it can improve the body's defence system and help a person combat disease more efficiently and effectively.

Sleep is the cheapest health aid a person can 'take'. Sleep is God's own means of restoring health to the body, as well as providing rest to the mind. Many have reported a new outlook or a change of heart after a good night's sleep.

Ask God to renew your strength as you sleep tonight . . . then go to bed on time so He can give you what you requested!

It is good to remember
that the tea kettle,
although up to its
neck in hot water,
continues to sing.

*Rejoice evermore. . . . In everything give
thanks: for this is the will of God in Christ
Jesus concerning you.*
1 Thessalonians 5:16,18 AV

Bernard Gilpin was accused of heresy before Bishop Bonner, and shortly afterwards was sent to London for trial. Gilpin's favourite saying was, 'All things are for the best.' He set out on his journey with that attitude, but on his way fell from his horse and broke his leg.

'Is all for the best now?' a bystander asked, mocking Gilpin for his optimism. 'I still believe so,' he replied.

He turned out to be right. During the time he was convalescing from the accident, and before he was able to resume his journey, Queen Mary died. Consequently, the case against him was dropped. Instead of being burned at the stake, Gilpin returned home in triumph.

We tend to see all accidents and illness that come our way as misfortune caused by the enemy of our souls. That may not always be the case. Rather than spend our energy railing against bad times, perhaps we should direct our effort towards praising the One who promises to work all things together for the good of those who are called according to His purposes (Romans 8:28). God has many methods and means for accomplishing His plan!

It's good to be a Christian
and know it,
but it's better
to be a Christian
and show it!

*By this all men will know that you are my
disciples, if you love one another.*
John 13:35 NIV

Before the colonialists imposed national boundaries, the kings of Laos and Vietnam had already reached an agreement about who was Laotian and who was Vietnamese. Those who ate short-grain rice, built their houses on stilts and decorated their homes with Indian-style serpents were considered Laotians. Those who ate long-grain rice, built their houses on the ground, and decorated their homes with Chinese-style dragons were Vietnamese. The king taxed the people accordingly and had little use for 'boundaries' apart from this designation.

The kings knew it was not the exact location of a person's home that determined their culture or loyalty. Instead, each person belonged to the kingdom whose values they shared.

So it is with a Christian. Regardless of our culture or nationality, we belong to God's kingdom. We live according to the values, standards and commandments He has established. When we pray, 'Thy kingdom come, Thy will be done', we are asking that the heavenly law of love might become established in our lives here on earth. We are His people, regardless of our address.

Sorrow looks back.
Worry looks around.
Faith looks up.

*Fixing our eyes on Jesus, the author and
perfector of faith, who for the joy set
before Him endured the cross, despising
the shame, and has sat down at the right
hand of the throne of God.*
Hebrews 12:2 NASB

Can the Lord speak through a pop song? Fontella Bass thinks so. She was at the lowest ebb in her life during 1990. It had been twenty-five years since her rhythm-and-blues single had hit number one in the charts. She had no career to speak of, and she was broke, tired and cold. The only heat in her house came from a gas stove in the kitchen. She had also strayed far from the church where she started singing gospel songs as a child.

Fontella says, 'I said a long prayer. I said, "I need to see a sign to continue on." ' No sooner had she prayed than she heard her hit song, 'Rescue Me', on a television commercial! To her, it was as if 'the Lord had stepped right into my world!'

Fontella was unaware American Express had been using her song as part of a commercial and officials had been unable to locate her to pay royalties. Not only did she receive back-royalties, but new opportunities began to open for her to sing.

She released a new album entitled *No Ways Tired*, but the best news is that she renewed her relationship with God. 'For many years I tried doing it on my own, and it didn't work,' she says. 'Then I took it out of my hands and turned it over to Him, and now everything's happening.'[13]

Sometimes we are so busy
adding up our troubles
that we forget to
count our blessings.

I will remember the works of the LORD;
Surely I will remember Your wonders of old.
I will also meditate on all Your work,
And talk of Your deeds.
Psalm 77:11,12 NKJ

In some parts of Mexico, hot springs and cold springs are found side by side. Because of this natural phenomenon, local women have the convenience of boiling their clothes in the hot springs, then rinsing them in the adjacent cold springs. While watching this procedure a number of years ago, a tourist said to her guide, 'I imagine that they think old Mother Nature is pretty generous to supply such ample, clean hot and cold water here side by side for their free use.'

The guide replied, 'Well, actually, no. There is much grumbling because Mother Nature supplies no soap! And not only that, but the rumour has started to filter in that there are machines that do this work in other parts of the world.'

So often we compare our lives to others – what they have in contrast to what we don't have and what they are that we aren't. Such comparisons invariably leave us feeling left out, rejected and cheated. If we are not careful to put the brakes on such negative emotions, we can become unnecessarily bitter.

Count your blessings today! If you own one, start with . . . a washing machine.

God can heal
a broken heart,
but He has to have
all the pieces

My son, give me your heart.
Proverbs 23:26 NKJ

So many things of beauty begin as 'bits and pieces' – not unlike our lives, which often seem like jigsaw puzzles with a multitude of scattered pieces.

Or the artist's collage.

Or a stained-glass window.

Or a mosaic floor.

Tragedies and pain can strike anyone, and we need to allow the Master Craftsman to put us back together according to His design, rather than trying to find all the pieces and glue ourselves together without Him.

In *The Dark Night of the Soul*, Georgia Harkness writes, 'The Christian faith imparts meaning to life. A living faith that is centred in God as revealed in Christ takes our chaotic, disorganised selves, with their crude jumble of pleasures and pains, and knits them together with a steadiness and joy that can endure anything with God.'[14]

Trust God today to turn your brokenness into something of beauty and value.

Be more concerned
with what God thinks
about you
than what people
think about you.

*But seek first the kingdom of God
and His righteousness,
and all these things shall be added to you.*
Matthew 6:33 NKJ

A pastor's wife was amazed when she heard someone say, 'One hour is only 4 per cent of the day.' She had not thought about time in this way. Sensing the need for more prayer time in her life, she thought surely she could give God at least 4 per cent of her time. She determined to try it.

Rather than try to fit prayer into her schedule, she decided to fix a prayer time, and then fit the rest of the day around it. At the time, her children were old enough to travel to school alone. By 8.30 each morning, a hush fell over her home. She knew her best hour for prayer would be between 8.30 and 9.30 a.m. To guarantee she was uninterrupted, she made it known in the parish that, except for emergencies, she would be grateful if people didn't call her until after 9.30 in the morning.

To her surprise, no one in the church was offended. Instead they responded very positively. Several other women began to follow her example by setting aside the same hour to pray every day!

When we seek God's plan *first*, all our plans with other people will have a way of falling into place.

The best way to get the last word is to apologise.

If you have been trapped by what
you said, ensnared by the words of
your mouth, then do this, my son,
to free yourself, since you have fallen
into your neighbour's hands:
Go and humble yourself;
press your plea with your neighbour!
Proverbs 6:2,3 NIV

In 1755, a 23-year-old colonel was in the midst of running for a seat in the Virginia assembly when he made an insulting remark in his campaign speech. The remark was addressed to a hot-tempered man named Payne, who responded by knocking the colonel down with a hickory stick. Soldiers rushed to the colonel's assistance, and it appeared that a full-blown fight would ensue. But the would-be politician got up, dusted himself off, called off the soldiers and left the scene.

The next morning the colonel wrote to Payne, requesting his presence at a local tavern. Payne obliged, but wondered what motives and demands the colonel might make – perhaps an apology or even a duel. To Payne's surprise, the colonel met him with an apology, asking forgiveness for his derogatory remarks and offering a handshake.

The move may have been viewed by others as politically expedient, but Colonel George Washington considered it personally imperative if he were to enjoy internal peace as he continued with his campaign.

The moment we feel like demanding forgiveness from others . . . may be the moment when we are to forgive.

Forget yourself for others and others will not forget you!

Treat other people exactly as you would like to be treated by them – this is the meaning of the Law and the Prophets.

Matthew 7:12 JBP

Millie was a mentally-retarded adult who lived with her mother in a small town. She was known for her proverbial 'green thumb' as a gardener. Lawns, hedges and flower beds flourished under her loving attention. Millie also did volunteer work by cutting grass, weeding, raking leaves and planting flowers in vacant lots throughout the town. She was known for her 'oil can': she always carried a small can of lubricating oil in her hip pocket and applied a dose of oil to any squeaky door, hinge or gate she encountered.

On Sundays, Millie went to church with her mother. When teased, she refused to respond in any way other than with good humour and unflappable cheer.

When Millie died, everyone in town showed up for her funeral. There were scores who travelled from distant places to attend, including many of those who had once teased her.

Without consciously attempting to do so, Millie exemplified good citizenship. She worked hard, was an optimist, eased tensions and was a faithful church member.

Others really do notice the small things we do for them in love and kindness.

The secret of
contentment is
the realization
that life is a gift,
not a right.

*But godliness with contentment is
great gain. For we brought nothing
into this world, and it is certain
we can carry nothing out.*
1 Timothy 6,7 AV

Former nationally syndicated columnist and current author, Anna Quindlen, seems to have enjoyed success at everything she has attempted. But in taking a fellow commentator to task after he made light of teenage problems, Anna was reminded of the two attempts to end her own life she had made at age sixteen. She writes, 'I was really driven through my high school years. I always had to be perfect in everyway, ranging from how I looked to how my grades were. It was too much pressure.'

In the early 1970s, Anna's mother died from ovarian cancer. This tragedy cured Anna from any desire to commit suicide. Her attitude towards life changed. 'I could never look at life as anything but a great gift. I realised I didn't have any business taking it for granted.'[16]

It is only when we recognise life as 'temporary' that we truly come to grips with what is important. When we face our own immortality, our priorities quickly come into focus. Consider your life as God's gift to you. Every moment is precious, so cherish each one. In doing so, you'll find purpose and meaning for each day.

Those who bring sunshine
to the lives of others
cannot keep it
from themselves.

Do not be deceived; God is not mocked,
for whatever a man sows,
that he will also reap.
Galatians 6:7 RSV

There was a wealthy noblewoman who had grown tired of life. She had everything one could wish for except happiness and contentment. She said, 'I am weary of life. I will go to the river and there end my life.'

As she walked along, she felt a little hand tugging at her skirts. Looking down, she saw a frail, hungry-looking little boy who pleaded, 'There are six of us. We are dying for want of food!' The noblewoman thought, *Why should I not relieve this wretched family? I have the means, and it seems I will have no more use for riches when I am gone.*

Following the little boy, she entered a scene of misery, sickness and want. She opened her purse and emptied its contents. The family members were beside themselves with joy and gratitude. Even more taken with their need, the noblewoman said, 'I'll return tomorrow and I will share with you more of the good things which God has given to me in abundance!'

She left that scene of want and wretchedness rejoicing that the child had found her. For the first time in her life she understood the reason for her wealth. Never again did she think of ending her life, which was now filled with meaning and purpose.

It's the little things in life
that determine
the big things.

'You have been faithful with a few things;
I will put you in charge of many things.
Come and share your master's happiness!'
Matthew 25:21 NIV

In speaking to a group of ministers, Fred Craddock noted the importance of being faithful in the little things of life. He added: 'To give my life for Christ appears glorious. To pour myself out for others . . . to pay the ultimate price of martyrdom – I'll do it. I'm ready, Lord, to go out in a blaze of glory.

'We think giving our all to the Lord is like taking a $1,000 bill and laying it on the table – "Here's my life, Lord. I'm giving it all."

'But the reality for most of us is that He sends us to the bank and has us cash in the $1,000 for quarters. We go through life putting out 25 cents here and 50 cents there. Listen to the neighbour's kid's troubles instead of saying "Get lost". Go to a committee meeting. Give a cup of water to a shaky old man in a nursing home.

'Unusually giving our life to Christ isn't glorious. It's done in all those little acts of love, 25 cents at a time. It would be easy to go out in a flash of glory; it's harder to live the Christian life little by little over the long haul.'[16]

Ask the Lord to show you how you can spend your life well.

Contentment isn't getting
what wc want
but being satisfied
with what we have.

Not that I complain of want;
for I have learned, in whatever state I am,
to be content.
Philippians 4:11 RSV

In a matter of seconds, Vickie's life was shattered. A trapeze artist, she lost control of the bar one day and fell head first into the net. She broke her neck between the fifth and sixth cervical vertebrae and became paralysed, a quadriplegic.

Three years after the accident, she had fallen into deep despair and self-pity and was determined to take her life. Her attempt failed, and she ended up in a psychiatric hospital. On the fourth anniversary of her fall, she and her husband separated. Bitterness set in.

One day a Christian home help was assigned to her. Mae Lynne introduced Vickie to Jesus Christ and the Bible. Vickie began to learn to 'stand firm' in her faith and to 'walk' in obedience to God.

A minister faithfully taught her for two years. Then Vickie began a ministry of encouragement by writing a dozen letters each week to prison inmates and others with disabilities. She now says, 'Quadriplegics aren't supposed to have this much joy, are they?'[17]

Vickie still uses a wheelchair, becomes dizzy at times, has occasional respiratory problems and needs a helper's care. However, she has deep inner strength because of her relationship with Jesus. Now others describe her as a 'fountain of smiles'.

God plus one is always a majority!

If God be for us, who can be against us?
Romans 8:31 AV

Cardinal von Faulhaber of Munich is reported once to have had a conversation with the famed physicist, Albert Einstein.

'Cardinal von Faulhaber,' Einstein said, 'I respect religion, but I believe in mathematics. Probably it is the other way around with you.'

'You are mistaken,' replied the Cardinal. 'To me, both are merely different expressions of the same divine exactness.'

'But, your Eminence, what would you say if mathematical science should some day come to conclusions directly contradictory to religious beliefs?'

'Oh,' the Cardinal answered with ease, 'I have the highest respect for the competence of mathematicians. I am sure they would never rest until they discovered their mistake.'

Regardless of how ardently some people try to suppress it, God's truth will always prevail!

Whoever gossips
to you
will be a gossip
of you.

A talebearer reveals secrets,
But he who is of a faithful spirit
conceals a matter.
Proverbs 11:13 NKJ

Laura Ingalls Wilder writes in *Little House in the Ozarks*: 'I know a little band of friends that calls itself a woman's club. The avowed purpose of this club is study, but there is an undercurrent of deeper, truer things than even culture and self-improvement. There is no obligation and there are no promises; but in forming the club and in selecting new members, only those are chosen who are kind-hearted and dependable as well as the possessors of a certain degree of intelligence and a small amount of that genius which is the capacity for careful work. In short, those who are taken into membership are those who will make good friends, and so they are a little band who are each for all and all for each . . .

'They are getting so in the habit of speaking good words that I expect to see them all develop into Golden Gossips.

'Ever hear of golden gossip? I read of it some years ago. A woman who was always talking about her friends and neighbours made it her *business* to talk of them, in fact, never to say anything but *good* of them. She was a gossip, but it was "golden gossip". This woman's club seems to be working in the same way.'[18]

Who wouldn't enjoy belonging to such a club?

Jesus is a friend who knows all your faults and still loves you anyway.

But God demonstrates His own love toward us, in that while we were still sinners, Christ died for us.

Romans 5:8 NKJ

At a crucial transition time, a Christian woman cried out to the Lord, despairing over the lack of spiritual power and fruitfulness she was experiencing in her life. Suddenly she sensed Jesus standing beside her, asking, 'May I have the keys to your life?'

The experience was so realistic, the woman reached into her pocket and took out a ring of keys. 'Are all the keys here?' the Lord asked.

'Yes, except the key to one small room in my life.'

'If you cannot trust Me in all rooms in your life, I cannot accept any of the keys.'

The woman was so overwhelmed at the thought of the Lord moving out of her life altogether, she cried, 'Lord . . . take the keys to all the rooms in my life!'

Many of us have rooms we hope no one will ever see. We intend to clean them out someday, but 'someday' never seems to come. When we invite Jesus into these rooms, He will help us clean them. With Him, we have the courage to throw away all the 'junk' and fill the rooms with His love and peace and joy.

Every person
should have a special
cemetery lot in which to
bury the faults of
friends and loved ones.

Be kind to each other, tenderhearted,
forgiving one another, just as God has
forgiven you because you belong to Christ.
Ephesians 4:32 TLB

A much-loved minister of God once carried a secret burden of long-past sin buried deep in his heart. He had committed the sin many years before during his seminary training. No one knew what he had done, but they did know he had repented. Even so, he had suffered years of remorse over the incident without any sense of God's forgiveness.

A woman in his church deeply loved God and claimed to have visions in which Jesus Christ spoke to her. The minister, sceptical of her claims asked her, 'The next time you speak to the Lord, will you please ask Him what sin your minister committed while he was in seminary.' The woman agreed.

When she came to the church a few days later the minister asked, 'Did He visit you?' She said, 'Yes.'

'And did you ask Him what sin I committed in seminary?'

'Yes, I asked Him,' she replied.

'Well, what did He say?'

'He said, "I don't remember." '

A minute of thought
is worth more than
an hour of talk.

Set a watch, O LORD, before my mouth;
keep the door of my lips.

Psalm 141:3 AV

A cardiologist was amazed at the great improvement one of his patients had made. When he had seen the woman a few months earlier, she was seriously ill in the hospital, needing an oxygen mask. He asked her what had happened.

The woman said, 'I was sure the end was near and that you and your staff had given up hope. However, on Thursday morning when you entered with your troops, something happened that changed everything. You listened to my heart; you seemed pleased by the findings, and you announced to all those standing about my bed that I had a 'wholesome gallop'. I knew that the doctors, in talking to me, might try to soften things. But I knew they wouldn't kid each other. So when I overheard you tell your colleagues I had a wholesome gallop, I figured I still had a lot of kick to my heart and could not be dying. My spirits were for the first time lifted, and I knew I would live and recover.'

The doctor never told the woman that a third-sound gallop is a poor sign that denotes the heart muscle is straining and usually failing!

Just a few words can be enough to make a difference in a person's life. How important it is to choose our words wisely!

You can win more friends
with your ears than
with your mouth.

Let every man be swift to hear,
slow to speak, slow to wrath.
James 1:19 AV

Dale Carnegie, author of *How to Win Friends and Influence People*, is considered one of the greatest 'friend winners' of the century. He taught, 'You can make more friends in two months by becoming interested in other people than you can in two years by trying to get other people interested in you.'

To illustrate his point, Carnegie would tell how dogs have learned the fine art of making friends better than most people. When you get within ten feet of a friendly dog, he will begin to wag his tail, a visible sign that he welcomes and enjoys your presence. If you take time to pet the dog, he will become excited, lick you and jump all over you to show how much he appreciates you. The dog becomes man's best friend by being genuinely interested in people!

One of the foremost ways, of course, in which we show our interest in others is to listen to them – to ask questions, intently listen to their answers, and to ask further questions based upon what they say. The person who feels 'heard' is likely to seek out his friendly listener again and again, and to count that person as a great friend.

Need a friend? Start listening to your heart.

It's not the outlook
but the uplook
that counts.

Looking unto Jesus
the author and finisher of our faith . . .
Hebrews 12:2 AV

The story of Helen Keller is well known. Deaf and blind from a childhood disease, her teacher, Anne Sullivan, opened the world to her through the other senses of taste, touch and smell. In her autobiography, Helen Keller wrote:

'Fate – silent, pitiless – bars the way. Fain would I question his imperious decree; for my heart is undisciplined and passionate, but my tongue will not utter the bitter, futile words that rise to my lips, and they fall back into my heart like unshed tears. Silence sits immense upon my soul. Then comes hope with a smile and whispers, "There is joy in self-forgetfulness." So I try to make the light in other people's eyes my sun, the music in others' ears my symphony, the smile on other's lips my happiness.'

How sad it is when we search only within ourselves for a reason to be happy, because the happiness in those around us tis reason enough to have joy, regardless of our situation or handicap. And, if the poor and the handicapped can have joy, how can we wallow in depression?

If we look to Jesus, all will be well with us . . . inside and out.

It isn't hard to make
a mountain out of
a molehill.
Just add a little dirt.

*Starting a quarrel is like breaching
a dam; so drop the matter
before a dispute breaks out.*
Proverbs 17:14 NIV

Susan was deeply disappointed at the lack of emotional closeness she felt in her marriage. She began to lash out at her husband. He, of course, reacted with his own defensive anger. Over time their anger grew, threats wre exchanged, and eventually divorce became part of their confrontations. Finally, Susan's husband moved out and she filed for divorce.

The divorce proceedings were bitter. They fought all the way through. When they met to sign the final papers, they stopped to look at each other and Susan saw in his eyes the very feelings she was experiencing – a feeling of longing and yet resignation. She thought, *I don't want to divorce him, and I don't think he wants to divorce me.*

She voiced her thoughts to her husband and for a moment it appeared he might soften and admit he too still cared. But then he said in a dull monotone, 'We've come this far, I guess we should finish it.' Susan left the courtroom realising she had never really wanted a divorce. She just wanted her husband to listen.

Don't allow anger to lead you anywhere . . . but especially down a road you truly don't want to travel.

The art of being a good guest is knowing when to leave.

Don't visit your neighbours too often; they may get tired of you and come to hate you.

Proverbs 25:17 GNB

It has been said that fish and house guests have one thing in common – after three days they both begin to stink. Depending on the circumstances, a stay may not require that much time before it 'goes bad'. Generally speaking, the more your hostess has put herself out on your account, the shorter your stay should be. Be certain before you visit with relatives or friends that you both know when you will arrive and when you will leave. The old entertainer's rule of thumb, 'Leave them wanting more' is good advice for a guest.

The same goes for shorter visits – better to leave earlier than later. When the hostess begins to yawn or gather up the dishes, take the hint!

George Washington visited the home of friends one evening, and when the hour came for him to leave, he said good-bye to the adults, then paused at the entrance where a little girl opened the door to let him out. Washington bowed to her and said, 'I am sorry, my little dear, to give you so much trouble.'

She replied, 'I wish, sir, it was to let you in.' Now that's a welcome guest!

Jesus is a friend who
walks in
when the world has
walked out.

*'I have told you all this so that you may
find your peace in me. You will find
trouble in the world – but, never lose
heart, I have conquered the world!'*
John 16:33 JBP

While serving in India, a devout English judge befriended a young Indian man. Having been raised in a prominent Indian family, he had been cast out after he had converted to Christianity. The judge took the boy into his household where he happily worked as a houseboy.

It was the custom of the household to have a devotional time every evening. One night the judge read aloud the words of Jesus: 'Every one that hath forsaken houses, or brethren, or sisters, or father, or mother, or wife, or children, or lands, for my name's sake, shall receive an hundredfold' (Matthew 19:29).

The judge turned to the lad and said, 'Nobody here has done this except you, Norbudur. Will you tell us, is it true what Jesus has said?'

The young Indian man read the verse aloud for himself and then turned to the family and said, 'No, there is an error.'

Startled, the judge responded, 'There is?'

The youth replied, 'It says He gives a hundredfold. I know He gives a thousandfold.'

With eternal life, intimacy with the Father and all the riches of heaven, who can truly measure the value of what it means when Jesus Christ comes into a person's life?

Those who deserve love the least need it the most.

But I say to you, love your enemies, bless those who curse you, do good to those who hate you, and pray for those who spitefully use you and persecute you.

Matthew 5:44 NKJ

On their way back from a meeting of the Greek Orthodox Archdiocese, Father Demetrios Frangos and Father Germanos Stavropoulos were in a car accident. A young woman high on drugs drove into their car while they waited at a stop light and both priests were killed instantly. The woman, a legal secretary with a seven-year-old daughter, had no previous police record, but admitted to having used drugs for ten years. She was charged with murder and several other felonies. The tabloid headlines were especially vicious, referring to her as the 'priest killer'.

Father Demetrios' son, George, responded with forgiveness, not anger. He offered to help provide the woman with a lawyer and hoped if she was convicted the sentence would be short. He said, 'The last thing my father would have wanted was to make an example [of her]. This woman is anguished and troubled to begin with . . . we have to look after the innocent one, the child. It is extremely important that the child be told that we forgive her mother.'[19]

George Frangos loved his father and grieved for him, but more important to him than 'legal justice' was 'divine justice' – that this woman and her little daughter know the love of Jesus Christ.

Faith is daring the soul
to go beyond
what the eyes can see.

For we walk by faith, not by sight.
2 Corinthians 5:7 AV

Sometimes I'm sad. I know not why
My heart is sore distressed;
It seems the burdens of this world
Have settled on my heart.
And yet I know . . . I know that God
Who doeth all things right
Will lead me thus to understand
To walk by FAITH . . . not SIGHT.
And though I may not see the way
He's planned for me to go . . .
That way seems dark to me just now
But oh, I'm sure He knows!
Today He guides my feeble step
Tomorrow's in His right . . .
He has asked me to never fear . . .
But walk by FAITH . . . not SIGHT.
Some day the mists will roll away,
The sun will shine again.
I'll see the beauty in the flowers.
I'll hear the bird's refrain.
An then I'll know my Father's hand
Has led the way to light
Because I placed my hand in His
And walked by FAITH . . . not SIGHT.

                    Ruth A. Morgan[20]

A critical spirit
is like poison ivy –
it only takes a little
contact to spread
its poison.

But avoid worldly and empty chatter,
for it will lead to further ungodliness.
2 Timothy 2:16 NASB

A little girl once asked her father how wars got started.

'Well,' said her father, 'suppose America persisted in quarrelling with England, and . . .'

'But,' interrupted her mother, 'America must never quarrel with England.'

'I know,' said the father, 'but I am only using a hypothetical instance.'

'But you are misleading the child,' protested Mum.

'No, I am not,' replied the father indignantly, with an edge of anger in his tone.

'Never mind, Daddy,' the little girl interjected, 'I think I know how wars get started.'

Most major arguments don't begin large, but are rooted in a small annoyance, breach or trespass. It's like the mighty oak that stood on the skyline of the Rocky Mountains. The tree had survived hail, heavy snows, bitter cold and ferocious storms for more than a century. It was finally felled not by a great lightning strike or an avalanche, but by an attack of tiny beetles.

A little hurt, neglect or insult can be the beginning of the end for virtually any relationship. Therefore, take care what you say and be certain the attitude you have is right!

Two things are hard
on the heart –
running up stairs and
running down people.

*Do not let any unwholesome talk
come out of your mouths, but only what
is helpful for building others up
according to their needs, that it may
benefit those who listen.*
Ephesians 4:29 NIV

W ouldn't this world be better,
    If folks whom we met would say,
'I know something good about you',
And treat you just that way?
Wouldn't it be splendid,
If each handshake, good and true,
Carried with it this assurance:
'I know something good about you'?
Wouldn't life be happier,
If the good that's in us all,
Were the only thing about us
That people would recall?
Wouldn't our days be sweeter,
If we praised the good we see?
For there is a lot of goodness,
In the worst of you and me.
Wouldn't it be fine to practise,
This way of thinking too;
You know something good about me,
I know something good about you?[21]

Since we can never know or tell the full story about
any other human being, why not just skip to the good
highlights?

Humour is to life what
shock absorbers are
to automobiles.

*Then our mouth was filled with laughter,
and our tongue with singing. Then they
said among the nations, 'The LORD has
done great things for them.'*
Psalm 126:2 NKJ

On a hot June day, Winona and Will had just exchanged their wedding vows and were about to take their triumphant wedding march back down the aisle. Suddenly Winona's six-foot-tall brother – a sidesman – fainted, and not very delicately at that. In the course of his falling, he toppled another sidesman and lurched against the best man, nearly forcing him down too. Two attendants each grabbed an arm of the fallen man and dragged him out of the church, in full view of the 300 guests and a horrified young bride.

Winona had no doubt her wedding was ruined and she would be the laughing stock of the town. It was all she could do to keep back the tears as she walked down the aisle with Will. As they neared the back of the church, however, Will burst into laughter – a big, booming, infectious laugh – and Winona had to laugh too. Soon the entire church was guffawing with gusto.

Winona said many years later, 'My first reaction to nearly any situation used to be "Oh, no", but Will's first reaction has always been to see humour in a situation. I've grown to adopt his point of view. I figure the very least I can glean from a nightmare is a good laugh and a memorable story to tell later.'[22]

Kindness is the oil that takes the friction out of life.

But the fruit of the Spirit is . . . kindness.
Galatians 5:22 NIV

A number of years ago, the Advertising and Sales Executive Club sponsored a Courtesy Campaign in Kansas City. One thousand silver dollars were flown in from Denver. Then, over a period of days, 'mystery shoppers' visited all types of stores, banks and other places of business. They listened to telephone operators and observed bus and street-car drivers. Each day they filed a written report on the persons they found to be the most courteous.

Those chosen as the most courteous people in the city received a silver dollar, along with a 'courtesy pays' button and a congratulatory card. The fifteen most outstandingly courteous people were guests at a banquet, where they were awarded $25 each. In all, more than 100 people were honoured.

What resulted was not only a temporary increase in the courtesy of local residents, but an awareness throughout the city that simple kindness is a pleasant thing with which to live! The 'residual effect' remained long after the campaign, to the point where Kansas City is still regarded as one of the friendliest cities in the nation.

It doesn't cost anything to be kind, but kindness can pay off in big ways quite apart from money.

Our days are identical
suitcases – all the
same size – but
some people can
pack more into them
than others.

*Be very careful, then, how you live – not
as unwise but as wise,
making the most of every opportunity.*
Ephesians 5:15,16 NIV

Mary Smith went to church one Sunday morning and winced when she heard the organist miss a note during the processional. She noted a teenager talking while everybody was supposed to be in prayer. She also couldn't help but notice that several flowers in the altar bouquets were wilted. She felt the usher was scrutinising what every person was putting into the offering plate, which made her angry. She counted at least five grammatical errors made by the preacher in his sermon. As she left the church through the side door after the closing hymn, she thought, *What a careless group of people!*

Amy Jones went to church one Sunday morning and was thrilled at the arrangement she heard of 'A Mighty Fortress'. Her heart was touched at hearing a teenager read the morning Scripture passage. She was encouraged to see the church take up an offering to help hungry children in Nigeria. The preacher's sermon answered a question that had bothered her for some time. She felt radiant joy from the choir members during the recessional. She left the church thinking, *What a wonderful place to worship God!*

Mary and Amy went to the same church, on the same Sunday morning.

To forgive is to set a
prisoner free and
discover the
prisoner was *you*.

*Your heavenly Father will forgive you if
you forgive those who sin against you;
but if you refuse to forgive them,
he will not forgive you.*
Matthew 6:14,15 TLB

Meredith was surprised to receive a letter from her brother, Tim. It had been three years since she had spoken to him, even though they lived in the same town. In the letter, Tim told her he and his wife were expecting twins and he hoped she would come to visit the babies after they were born. He expressed his sorrow that they had not communicated more, and apologised for whatever it was he had done to cause them to be estranged.

Meredith's initial reaction was one of anger. *'Whatever it was'? Didn't he know?* She immediately sat down and wrote a five-page letter detailing all the wrongs Tim had committed that hurt her. The phone rang, however, before she could put her letter in an envelope, and it was several hours before she returned to her writing desk. Upon rereading her letter, she was horrified at what she found.

She had thought she was being very matter of fact, but her words were full of anger and pain. Tears of forgiveness filled her eyes. *Perhaps it wasn't all Tim's fault.*

She called him the next day to say, 'I can hardly wait to be the aunt of twins!'

The heart is the happiest when it beats for others.

'Greater love has no one than this, than to lay down one's life for his friends.'
John 15:13 NKJ

Albert Einstein once reflected on the purpose of man's existence: 'Strange is our situation here upon earth. Each of us comes for a short visit, not knowing why, yet sometimes seeming to a divine purpose. From the standpoint of daily life, however, there is one thing we do know: that we are here for the sake of others . . . for the countless unknown souls with whose fate we are connected by a bond of sympathy. Many times a day, I realise how much my own outer and inner life is built upon the labours of people, both living and dead, and how earnestly I must exert myself in order to give in return as much as I have received.'

When we truly take stock of our lives, we must admit we have done *nothing* solely on our own. Our thinking has been fashioned by our many teachers and mentors, including family members. Our ability to function physically is the result, in part, of our genetic code and the productivity of others in providing food, water and shelter. Our spiritual lives are a gift of God Himself. We are what we have received.

Our reaction to these facts drives each of us to give to others the good thing we have been fortunate to receive. That is what being a citizen of God's kingdom is all about!

A true friend never
gets in your way
unless you happen to
be going down.

*A friend loves at all times, and a brother is
born for adversity.*

Proverbs 17:17 NASB

One evening, when a woman was driving home, she noticed a truck driving very close behind her. She accelerated to put a little distance between them, but when she sped up, the truck did too. The faster she drove, the faster he drove.

Frightened at being pursued this way, she got off the motorway, but the truck followed her. She turned up a main road, hoping to lose him in traffic, but he even ran a red light in pursuit. Finally, near the point of panic, she pulled into a service station and bolted out of her car screaming for help. She was horrified to see the truck driver spring from his vehicle and run toward her.

But then . . . not even looking at her, he yanked open the back door of her car and pulled out a man who was hiding on the floor of her back seat.

Her pursuer had not been the real potential for danger in her life! The truck driver had spotted the man, a convicted rapist, leave a café and hide in her car shortly before she returned. His chase was not an effort to harm her, but to save her, even at the risk of his own life.

We often find true, faithful friends in those who have been close to us for years, but rarely in strangers.

Laughter is the brush
that sweeps away the
cobwebs of the heart.

A happy heart is a good medicine
and a cheerful mind works healing,
but a broken spirit dries the bones.
Proverbs 17:22 AMP

In *Growing Strong in the Seasons of Life*, Charles Swindoll writes: 'Tonight was fun 'n' games night around the supper table in our house. It was wild. First of all, one of the kids snickered during the prayer (which isn't that unusual) and that tipped the first domino. Then a humorous incident from school was shared and the event (as well as how it was told) triggered havoc around the table. That was the beginning of twenty to thirty minutes of the loudest, silliest, most enjoyable laughter you can imagine. At one point I watched my oldest literally fall off his chair in hysterics, my youngest doubled over in his chair as his face wound up on his plate with corn chips stuck to his cheeks . . . and my two girls leaning back, lost and preoccupied in the most beautiful and beneficial therapy God ever granted humanity: *laughter*.

'What is so amazing is that everything seemed far less serious and heavy. Irritability and impatience were ignored like unwanted guests. For example, during the meal little Chuck spilled his drink twice . . . and even *that* brought the house down. If I remember correctly, that made six times during the day he accidentally spilled his drink, but nobody bothered to count.'[23]

Laughter . . . what a treasure it is!

God has a history of using the insignificant to accomplish the impossible.

Jesus looked straight at them and answered, 'This is impossible for human beings, but not for God; everything is possible for God.'
Mark 10:27 GNB

In order to communicate among themselves, Serbian shepherd boys developed an ingenious system. They would stick the blades of their long knives into the ground of a pasture, and when one of the boys sensed an approaching cattle thief, he would strike the handle of his knife sharply. The vibration created a signal that could be picked up by other shepherd boys, their ears pressed tightly against the ground. It was by this unique system that they outwitted thieves who tried to creep up on their flocks and herds under the cover of darkness and tall corn.

Most of the shepherd boys grew up and forgot about their ground signals, but one boy remembered. Twenty-five years after he left the pastures, he made one of the greatest inventions of the modern era. Michael Pupin changed the telephone from a device used only to speak across a city, to a long-distance instrument that could be heard across a continent.

Something you take for granted today . . . something others may consider to be insignificant or ordinary . . . may actually become your key to greatness. Look around you. What is it that God has put at your disposal?

People may doubt
what you say,
but they will always believe
what you do.

*. . . for the tree is known and recognized
and judged by its fruit.*
Matthew 12:33 AMP

Y ou may bring to your office,
  and put in a frame,
a motto as fine as its paint,
but if you're a crook
when you're playing the game,
that motto won't make you a saint.
You can stick up the placards
all over the wall,
but here is a word I announce:
It is not the motto that hangs on the wall,
but the motto you live, that counts.
If the motto says, 'Smile,'
and you carry a frown:
'Do it now,' and you linger and wait;
if the motto says 'Help,'
and you trample men down;
if the motto says, 'Love,' and you hate –
you won't get away
with the mottoes you stall,
for truth will come forth with a bounce.
It is not the motto
that hangs on the wall,
but the motto you live, that counts.'[24]

Kindness
is a language
which the deaf can hear
and the blind can see.

For great is his love towards us,
and the faithfulness of the LORD endures
for ever. Praise the LORD.
Psalm 117:2 NIV

'I often have though that we are a little old-fashioned here in the Ozark hills,' writes Laura Ingalls Wilder in *Little House in the Ozarks*. 'Now I know we are, because we had a 'working' in our neighbourhood this winter. That is a blessed, old-fashioned way of helping out a neighbour.

'While the winter was warm, still it had been much too cold to be without firewood; and this neighbour, badly crippled with rheumatism, was not able to get up his winter's wood . . . So the men of the neighbourhood gathered together one morning and dropped in on him. With crosscut saws and axes, they took possession of his wood lot . . . By night there was enough wood ready . . . to last the rest of winter.

'The women did their part, too. All morning they kept arriving with well-filled baskets, and at noon a long table was filled with a country neighbourhood dinner . . . When the dishes were washed, they sewed, knit, crocheted and talked for the rest of the afternoon. It was a regular old-fashioned good time, and we all went home with the feeling expressed by a newcomer when he said, "Don't you know I'm proud to live in a neighbourhood like this where they turn out and help one another when it's needed." '25

I make it a rule
of Christian duty
never to go to a place
where there is not
room for my Master
as well as myself.

*Don't be teamed with those who do not
love the LORD . . . How can a Christian be
a partner with one who doesn't believe?*
2 Corinthians 6:14,15 TLB

An attractive single woman had a job that required her to travel a great deal. When a new female colleague was added to her department she told her how happy she was to have another woman on the team. She related how she often felt isolated when she found herself the only woman at breakfast in a hotel restaurant, or one of only a handful of women on a commuter flight.

'Do the men ever bother you?' the new young colleague asked.

'Rarely,' the woman replied.

'Wow,' said the young colleague. 'You are so beautiful, I would think you were approached a great deal by men you really don't care to meet.'

'No,' the woman explained, 'I just say five words and immediately I am left alone.'

'When I am approached by a man,' the woman continued, 'I simply ask, "Are you a born-again Christian?"'

'Has anyone ever said "yes"?' the younger asked.

'Rarely,' said the woman. 'And when such men want to talk to me anyway, I always have an enjoyable conversation, because Jesus can be part of it.'

Jesus can turn water
into wine,
but He can't turn
your whining
into anything.

*Do all things without murmurings
and disputings.*
Philippians 2:14 AV

Rather than whining that we don't have certain things in our lives or that something is wrong, we need to take positive action. Here are four steps towards turning whining into thanksgiving:

1. *Give something away.* When you give something you create both a physical and a mental space for something new and better to come into your life. Although you may think you are 'lacking' something in life, when you give you demonstrate you have abundance to spare.

2. *Narrow your goals.* Don't expect everything good to come into your life all at once. When you focus your expectations toward specific and reachable goals, you are more apt to direct your time and energy toward reaching them.

3. *Change your vocabulary from 'I need' to 'I want'.* Most of the things we think we need are actually things we want. When you receive them, you are more likely to be thankful for them as luxuries rather than necessities.

4. *Choose to be thankful for what you already have.* Thanksgiving is a choice we make. Every one of us has more things to be thankful for than we could begin to recount in a day.

The smallest deed
is better than
the greatest intention!

Let us not love [merely] in theory or in
speech but in deed and in truth –
in practice and in sincerity.
1 John 3:18 AMP

A missionary was sailing home on furlough when she heard a cry one night – a cry that is perhaps the most difficult to hear when at sea: 'Man overboard!' She arose quickly from her berth, lit the lamp on the bracket in her cabin, and then held the lamp at the window of her cabin in hopes of seeing some sign of life in the murky dark waters outside.

Seeing nothing, she hung the lamp back on its bracket, snuffed it out and returned to her berth with prayers for the man lost at sea. In the morning, to her surprise she discovered the man had been rescued. Not only that, but she learned it was the flash of her lamp through the porthole that showed those on deck the location of the missing man, who was clinging desperately to a rope still attached to the deck. He was pulled from the cold waters in the nick of time. Such a small deed as shining a lamp at the right time had saved a man's life.

It isn't the size of the deed you do that counts. It's the fact that you do it for good and not for evil, and with a trust that God can take every deed we perform and use it for His purposes, in our lives and in the lives of others.

I've suffered a great
many catastrophes
in my life.
Most of them
never happened.

For God hath not given us the spirit of
fear; but of power, and of love,
and of a sound mind.
2 Timothy 1:7 AV

A military chaplain once drew up a 'Worry Table' based upon the problems men and women had brought to him through his years of service. He found their worries fit into these categories:

Worries about things that never happened – 40%
Worries about past, unchangeable decisions – 30%
Worries about illness that never happened – 12%
Worries about adult children and friends (who
        were able to take care of themselves) – 10%
Worries about real problems – 8%

According to his chart, 92 per cent of all worries are about things we can't control, concerns which are better left to God. The truth is, most of our anxieties are rooted in a failure to trust God.

We simply don't believe He is big enough or cares enough to handle our problems, give us the desires of our hearts, and keep us – and our loved ones – from harm.

Knowing God's character, we can easily see how we worry for nothing most of the time!

Guilt is concerned
with the past.
Worry is concerned
about the future.
Contentment
enjoys the present.

*Not that I am implying that I was in any
personal want, for I have learned how to
be content (satisfied to the point where I
am not disturbed or disquieted)
in whatever state I am.*
Philippians 4:11 AMP

Psychologist William Marston once asked three thousand people, 'What have you to live for?' He was shocked to discover that 94 per cent of the people he polled were simply enduring the present while they waited for the future. Some indicated they were waiting for 'something' to happen – waiting for children to grow up and leave home, waiting for next year, waiting for another time to take a long-awaited trip, waiting for someone to died or waiting for tomorrow. They had hope, but no ongoing purpose to their lives!

Only 6 per cent of the people identified relationships and activities in the present tense of their lives that they counted as valuable reasons for living!

The 94 per cent would be wise to recall the words of this poem by an unknown author:

During all the years since time began,
Today has been the friend of man;
But in his blindness and his sorrow,
He looks to yesterday and tomorrow.
Forget past trials and your sorrow.
There was, but is, no yesterday,
And there may be no tomorrow.[26]

People with tact
have less to retract.

*The heart of the righteous
weighs its answers, but the mouth of the
wicked gushes evil.*
Proverbs 15:28 NIV

Birds sing . . . and never have to apologise for their songs.

Dogs bark and kittens meow . . . and never have to say, 'I'm sorry for what I just said.'

Lions roar and hyenas howl . . . but they never have to retract their statements as being untrue.

The fact is, the members of the animal kingdom are themselves, and they are true in their expression to what they were created to be.

Many times we human beings find ourselves embarrassed at our own words – feeling apologetic, caught in an awkward moment, or recognising we have spoken the wrong words at the wrong time – because we have begun evaluating the performance of others and develop a critical attitude.

The bluejay doesn't criticise the robin. The kitten doesn't make snide remarks about the puppy. The lion doesn't ridicule the hyena. In like manner, we should not put down others whom we can never fully understand, never fully appreciate, or never fully emulate.

Stick to singing your own song today and appreciate the uniqueness of those around you. You will easily avoid putting your foot in your mouth!

Being at peace
with yourself
is a direct result of
finding peace with God.

And the peace of God, which surpasses all understanding, will guard your hearts and minds through Christ Jesus.

Philippians 4:7 NKJ

Tom Dooley was a young doctor who gave up an easy career to organise hospitals and pour out his life in service to afflicted people in South-East Asia. As he lay dying of cancer aged thirty-four, Dooley wrote to the president of Notre Dame, his alma mater:

'Dear Father Hesburgh; They've got me down. Flat on the back, with plaster, sand bags and hot water bottles. I've contrived a way of pumping the bed up a bit so that, with a long reach, I can get to my typewriter . . . Two things prompt this note to you. The first is that whenever my cancer acts up a bit . . . I turn inward. Less do I think of my hospitals around the world. Or of 94 doctors, fund-raisers and the like. More do I think of one Divine Doctor and my personal fund of grace . . . I have monstrous phantoms; all men do. And inside and outside the wind blows. But when the time comes, like now, when the storm around me does not matter. The winds within me do not matter. Nothing human or earthly can touch me. A peace gathers in my heart. What seems unpossessable, I can possess. What seems unfathomable, I can fathom. What is unutterable, I can utter. Because I can pray. I can communicate. How do people endure anything on earth if they cannot have God?'[27]

If you want to make
an easy job seem mighty
hard, just keep
putting off doing it.

'How long are you going to wait before
you go in and take the land that the LORD,
the God of your ancestors, has given you?'
Joshua 18:3 GNB

When Beth's boss asked her to take on an extra project, Beth saw the opportunity to prove she could handle greater responsibility. She immediately began to think how she might approach the task and her enthusiasm ran high. But when the time came to start the project, Beth found herself telling her boss she was too busy to do the job justice. The project was given to someone else, who earned a promotion for completing it successfully. Beth didn't receive any new opportunities and eventually took a position with another firm.

What had kept Beth from doing the project? Simple procrastination. She put off getting started on the job until she was paralysed with fear – fear that she might not be able to do the job or that her performance would not meet her boss's expectation. In the end, Beth didn't move ahead and thus reinforced her fears with a bigger sense of insecurity about her own ability.

If you find yourself procrastinating, ask God to show you how to overcome your fear, then do what He says. He wants you to succeed and live a fulfilled life, but you must step out in faith for Him to bless you!

Love sees through
a telescope
not a microscope.

*Love endures long and is patient and kind
. . . it takes no account of the evil done to
it – pays no attention to a suffered wrong.*
1 Corinthians 13:4,5 AMP

On Christmas morning, little Amy was delighted to find a beautiful golden-haired doll among the presents she unwrapped. 'She's so pretty!' Amy squealed in excitement as she hugged her new doll. Then rushing to hug her grandmother, the giver of the doll, she cried 'Thank you, thank you, thank you!'

Amy played with her new doll most of the day, but towards evening, she put it down and sought out one of her old dolls. Amy cradled the tattered and dilapidated old doll in her arms. Its hair had nearly worn away, its nose was broken, one eye was askew and an arm was missing.

'Well, well,' Grandma noted, 'it seems as though you like that old dolly better.'

'I like the beautiful doll you gave me, Grandma,' little Amy explained, 'but I love this old doll more, because if I didn't love her, no one else would.'

We all know the saying, 'Beauty is in the eye of the beholder.' A similar saying might be, 'Love is the choice of the beholder.' When we see faults in others, we can choose to look beyond them. We can choose to love them regardless of their negative attributes, faults or quirks.

Life is not a problem
to be solved,
but a gift
to be enjoyed.

*This is the day the LORD has made; let us
rejoice and be glad in it.*

Psalm 118:24 NIV

The fictional character, Sherlock Holmes, is known for his keen power of observation in solving crimes. But Holmes also used his observation skills in renewing his faith. In *The Adventure of the Naval Treaty*, Dr Watson says of Holmes, 'He walked past the couch to an open window and held up the drooping stalk of a moss rose, looking down at the dainty blend of crimson and green. It was a new phase of his character to me, for I had never before seen him show an interest in natural objects.

' "There is nothing in which deduction is so necessary as in religion," said he, leaning with his back against the shutters . . . "Our highest assurance of the goodness of Providence seems to me to rest in the flowers. All other things, our powers, our desires, our food are really necessary for our existence in the first instance. But this rose is an extra. Its smell and its colour are an embellishment of life, not a condition of it. It is only goodness which gives extras and so I say again that we have much to hope from the flowers." '[28]

Life is filled with 'extras' – gifts from a loving God that embellish and enrich our lives. Take time to observe some of them today!

A pint of example
is worth
a barrelful of advice.

Join with others in following my example,
brothers, and take note of those who live
according to the pattern we gave you.
Philippians 3:17 NIV

On the fourth Sunday in July, the descendants of Roberto and Raquel Beaumont celebrate 'Offspring Day.' They have been doing this since 1956, when Raquel gathered her five pre-teen children around the dinner table at their home in Lima, Peru. She placed a rose by the napkin of each daughter and a carnation by the napkin of each son.

Knowing in a few years her children would be going their separate ways, she told them that the gifts she gave them on Offspring Day were not mere flowers, but a token of her true gift to them – time and love. Furthermore, she expected them to pass on those same gifts to their children. Through the years, Raquel was the best example of her message: she always had time and love for each of her children, who regularly sought her advice and encouragement.

On Offspring Day each year, the elders who gather offer words of wisdom to their children. The young are encouraged to pick one thing about themselves they hope to improve in the coming year. It is a time for the generations to hear from one another and to set new goals for relationships. They do it all in the spirit of 'Raquel's example'.

Beware lest your
footprints on the
sand of time
leave only the
marks of a heel.

*The memory of the righteous will be a
blessing, but the name of
the wicked will rot.*

Proverbs 10:7 NIV

In *Grand Essentials*, Ben Patterson writes: 'I have a theory about old age . . . I believe that when life has whittled us down, when joints have failed and skin has wrinkled . . . what is left of us will be what we were all along, in our essence.

'Exhibit A is a distant uncle . . . All his life he did nothing but find new ways to get rich . . . He spent his senescence very comfortably, drooling and babbling constantly about the money he had made . . . When life whittled him down to his essence, all there was left was raw greed.

'Exhibit B is my wife's grandmother . . . The best example I can think of was when we asked her to pray before dinner. She would reach out and hold the hands of those sitting beside her, a broad, beatific smile would spread across her face, her dim eyes would fill with tears as she looked up to heaven, and her chin would quaver as she poured out her love to Jesus. That was Edna in a nutshell. She loved Jesus and she loved people. She couldn't remember our names, but she couldn't keep her hands from patting us lovingly whenever we got near her. When life whittled her down to her essence, all there was left was love: love for God and love for people.'[29]

If you were given a nickname descriptive of your character, would you be proud of it?

A good name is rather to be chosen than great riches.
Proverbs 22:1 AV

In 1955, the city buses in Montgomery, Alabama, were segregated by law. White people and black people were not allowed to sit together.

On December 1 of that year, Mrs Rosa Parks was riding the bus home from her job at a tailor shop. As the section for whites filled up, the black people were ordered to move to the back to make room for the white passengers who were boarding. Three blacks in Mrs Parks' row moved, but Mrs Parks remained in her seat. Later she said, 'Our mistreatment was just not right and I was tired of it. I knew someone had to take the first step. So I made up my mind not to move.'

The bus driver asked if she was going to stand up.

'No, I am not,' she answered him. Mrs Parks was arrested and taken to jail. Four days later black people and white sympathisers organised a boycott of the city bus line that lasted until a year later, when the Supreme Court declared the segregated-bus ordinance unconstitutional.

Mrs Parks is known today as the 'mother of the modern-day civil rights movement'. Her name inspires others to be courageous and do what is right, despite the circumstances.

It's easy to identify people
who can't count to ten.
They're in front of you
in the supermarket
express lane.

Be patient with everyone.
1 Thessalonians 5:14 NIV

A woman once visited a friend in Cambridge, Massachusetts, home of several well-known institutions of higher learning. She accompanied the friend to a supermarket on Saturday afternoon, finding it crammed with shoppers and very long checkout lines.

While the two of them stood patiently in line, they noticed a college-age young man wheel a filled shopping cart into the cash register stall that was clearly marked, 'Express line – 8 items or less'.

The checkout girl of the express line looked at the loaded cart and then at the young man. He was trying to ignore her exasperated expression by fumbling for his chequebook in his knapsack.

Realising she was stuck with a stubborn and inconsiderate customer, the girl said loudly to the high school student who was helping her bag groceries, 'This guy either goes to Harvard and can't count, or he goes to MIT and can't read!'

Although we don't always think of it in these terms, impatience reveals a selfish and often mean spirit, while patience is really an act of kindness.

Tact is the art of making a point without making an enemy.

*Reckless words pierce like a sword but,
the tongue of the wise brings healing.*
Proverbs 12:18 NIV

In looking over a café menu, a woman noticed that both a chicken salad sandwich and a chicken sandwich were listed. She decided to order the chicken salad sandwich, but absent-mindedly wrote 'chicken sandwich' on her order slip. When the waiter brought the chicken sandwich, she protested immediately, insisting the waiter had erred.

Most waiters would have picked up the order slip and shown the customer the mistake she had made. But instead, he expressed regret at the error, picked up the sandwich, returned to the kitchen and a moment later placed a chicken salad sandwich in front of the woman.

While eating her sandwich, the woman picked up her order slip and noticed the mistake she had made. When it was time to pay for the meal, she apologised to the waiter and offered to pay for both sandwiches. The waiter said, 'No, ma'am. That's perfectly all right. I'm just happy you've forgiven me for being right.'

Silence is one of the hardest
arguments to refute.

*He who keeps his mouth and his tongue
keeps himself out of trouble.*
Proverbs 21:23 RSV

Ruth Bell Graham tells a humorous story about her daughters, Anne and Bunny. When Ruth ran to the kitchen to investigate some loud cries, she found three-year-old Bunny holding her hand to her cheek, looking very disapprovingly at her sister. 'Mummy,' explained five-year-old Anne, 'I'm teaching Bunny the Bible. I'm slapping her on one cheek and teaching her to turn the other one so I can slap it, too.'[30]

When we are wronged, our first response is more likely to fight back than to turn the other cheek. But many have found that fighting back can be counter-productive.

Missionary E. Stanley Jones was being publicly slandered by someone he had once helped. Jones' first response was to write his accuser a letter which he relates was 'the kind of reply you are proud of the first five minutes, the second five minutes you're not so certain and the third five minutes you know you're wrong'.

Jones knew his comments would win the argument, but lose the person. 'The Christian,' he said, 'is not in the business of winning arguments, but of winning people,' and he tore up the letter. A few weeks later – without having said a word – Jones received a letter of apology from the one who had turned on him.

The best antique is
an old friend.

Your own friend and your father's friend,
forsake not . . . Better is a neighbour who
is near [in spirit] than a brother who is far
off [in heart].
Proverbs 27:10 AMP

A woman was in a serious car accident in a city far from home. She felt so enclosed in a cocoon of pain, she didn't realise how lonely she was until a 'forgotten' friend in the city came to visit her. She firmly but gently said to her, 'You should not be alone.'

In the weeks that followed, this friend's advice rang in the injured woman's ears and helped her to overcome her otherwise reserved nature. When another friend called from a city several hundred miles away to say she wanted to come and stay with her, the injured woman didn't say, 'Don't bother' – as would have been her normal response. Rather, she said, 'Please come.' The friend was a wonderful encourager and nurse to her, reading the Psalms aloud when she was still too weak to read herself. Then yet another friend offered to come and help in her recovery. Again she swallowed her pride and said, 'Please do.' This friend stayed for several months until the injured woman was able to care for herself.

Even Jesus did not carry His own cross all the way to Calvary. He allowed another to help shoulder His burden. It's all right to ask for help and to receive help. You don't have to 'go it alone'. Let a friend help you!

If you can't feed
a hundred people
then just feed one.

*Therefore, as we have opportunity, let us
do good to all.*
Galatians 6:10 NKJ

When 13-year-old Bobby Hill, the son of a US Army sergeant stationed in Italy, read a book about the work of Nobel Prize winner Albert Schweitzer, he decided to do something to help the medical missionary. He sent a bottle of aspirin to Lieutenant General Richard C. Lindsay, Commander of the Allied air forces in Southern Europe, asking if any of his airplanes could parachute the bottle of aspirin to Dr Schweitzer's jungle hospital in Africa.

Upon hearing the letter, an Italian radio station issued an appeal, resulting in more than $400,000 worth of donated medical supplies. The French and Italian governments each supplied a plane to fly the medicines and the boy to Dr Schweitzer. The grateful doctor responded, 'I never thought a child could do so much for my hospital.'

None of us may be able to solve all the problems in the world, but we can feed a hungry family in a near-by neighbourhood, clothe the homeless person who has just arrived at a shelter, or give a blanket to a street person who lives near our office building. If every person who could offer help would take just one step every month to meet just one person's need, think what might be accomplished!

The trouble with
stretching the truth
is that it's apt
to snap back.

A false witness will not go unpunished,
and he who utters lies will escape.
Proverbs 19:5 RSV

A Sunday School teacher once told her adult class, 'Next Sunday I am going to teach a very important lesson. I want you all to read chapter 17 of St Mark's Gospel in preparation.' The members of the class nodded, indicating a willingness to do as the teacher requested.

The following Sunday the teacher asked the class, 'Those who read chapter 17 of St Mark's Gospel during this past week, please raise your hands.' Nearly all the people in the room raised their hands.

The teacher then said, 'That's very interesting. The Gospel of Mark has only sixteen chapters. But at least I know that my lesson is going to hit the mark. Today I'm going to teach what Jesus had to say about lying.'

Perhaps the greatest punishment for lying is not that a person gets caught in the lie, but rather, the 'hidden' punishment that a liar can never truly believe what anyone else says.

Tell the truth! You'll suffer far less embarrassment and be much healthier emotionally. Even if truth-telling brings temporary pain, God will honour your courage and bless you for doing the right thing.

Birthdays are good for you.
Statistics show that
the people who have the
most live the longest.

Teach us to number our days aright,
that we may gain a heart of wisdom.
Psalm 90:12 NIV

There once was a woman who, upon seeing her hair turn grey, decided she must be getting old. She immediately slowed her pace, refused to wear bright colours, tried to act more sedately and began to wear 'sensible shoes'. She let her hair grow long and put it up in a bun on her head, wore long sleeves to cover what she was sure must be unsightly 'old lady' arms, and could often be heard telling friends who asked her how she was doing, 'I suppose I'm doing as well as could be expected for a person my age.'

One day she overheard a teenager ask a friend, 'How old is Miss Tilly?' The friend said, 'Well, from the way she looks and acts, I'd say she's at least 65 to 70.' The woman was shocked – they were talking about her, and she was only 55! She decided she was looking far too old for her years and immediately shifted into reverse. Bright colours, high heels and more stylish clothes rejoined her closet. She cut her hair and used a rinse to colour the grey. Several months later, a 48-year-old man asked her out and wouldn't believe her when she told him her age.

She concluded, 'Fifty-five is a better speed limit than age limit.'

Faults are thick
where love is thin.

Above everything else be sure that you
have real deep love for each other,
remembering how love can 'cover
a multitude of sins'.
1 Peter 4:8 JBP

H *ave you ever noticed ...*
WHEN others are set in their ways, they're obstinate ... but you are firm and resolved.

WHEN your neighbour doesn't like your friend, she's prejudiced ... but when you don't like her friend, you're a good judge of human nature.

WHEN she tries to treat someone especially well, she's buttering up the person ... but when you do so, you're being thoughtful.

WHEN she takes time to do things well, she's lazy ... but when you do so, you're meticulous.

WHEN she spends a lot, she's a spendthrift ... but when you overdo, you're generous.

WHEN she picks flaws in things, she's critical ... but when you do so, you are perceptive.

WHEN she is mild-mannered, you call her weak ... but when you are, you're gracious.

WHEN she dresses well, she is extravagant ... but when you do, you're tastefully in style.

WHEN she says what she thinks, she's spiteful ... but when you do, you're being honest.

WHEN she takes great risks, she's foolhardy ... but when you do, you're brave.

The only way to have a friend is to be one.

A man who has friends
must himself be friendly.

Proverbs 18:24 NKJ

A young family in the 1950s had just purchased their first television set. All the neighbours gathered to help them put up the antenna on the roof of their home. Since they had only the simplest of tools, they weren't making much progress.

Then a new neighbour and his wife showed up with a large elaborate tool box, filled with just about every gadget or tool one could imagine. They had everything needed to install the antenna, which was set up in near record time after their arrival.

The group of volunteers immediately went inside to see what kind of reception their neighbours would get on their new television set. The picture was crystal clear! Success was theirs!

As the neighbours stood around congratulating themselves on their fine work, they thanked their new neighbours for their valuable assistance. One of the women asked, 'What is it that you make with such a well-equipped tool box?'

The new neighbours smiled sincerely and replied with genuine warmth, 'Friends.'

The world wants
your best
but God wants
your all.

*You shall love the Lord your God with all
your heart, and with all your soul, and
with all your mind.*
Matthew 22:37 RSV

Janette Oke, best-selling novelist with more than forty books to her credit, is considered the modern 'pioneer author' for Christian fiction. Her books have sold millions of copies since her first novel was published in 1979.

When she first decided to write, she said to God, 'Lord, I'm going to write this book. If it works, and if I discover I have talent, I'll give it all to You.'

Janette sensed God was not pleased with the bargain she was trying to strike with Him. She felt in her heart as if He was responding, 'If you're serious about this, then I want everything before you start.' Thus she gave Him her ambitions and dreams, and trusted Him with the outcome of her efforts. She left it up to Him to teach her, whether she was successful or not.

Out of that resolve came a second resolve. She refused to compromise her principles. Although she would write realistically, her stories would be 'wholesome and good and encouraging'. Many thought that approach was doomed to failure at the outset, but a shelf of novels later . . . Janette Oke has proved 'God can teach spiritual truths through fictional characters'.[31]

Hindsight explains
the injury
that foresight
would have prevented.

*Do not forsake wisdom, and she will
protect you . . . When you walk,
your steps will not be hampered; when
you run, you will not stumble.*
Proverbs 4:6,12 NIV

The mother of six children walked into her house one day to see all her children huddled together in a circle. She approached them to see what had evoked such intense interest, and she could hardly believe her eyes.

To her horror, in the middle of the circle of children were several baby skunks. She immediately screamed at the top of her voice, 'Children! Run, run, run! Out, out, out!'

At the sound of their mother's alarmed voice, each child quickly grabbed a baby skunk and headed for the door. The screaming and panic, of course, set off the instinctive danger alarm in the skunks, and each of them quickly dispelled its horrible scent. Each child and the house itself were doused with an aroma that lingered for weeks, regardless of intense scrubbing and use of disinfectants.

How we react has greater negative consequences than the initial negative situation we encounter! Don't make matters worse by unplanned, emotion-driven, spur-of-the-moment behaviour. Choose to act rather than to react, taking sufficient time to select a course of action based upon calm reason and thoughtful prayer.

Do not in the
darkness of night,
what you'd shun in
broad daylight.

The night is far spent, the day is at hand:
let us therefore cast off the works of
darkness, and let us put on
the armour of light.
Romans 13:12 AV

Herbert V. Prochnow has constructed a ten-part 'Character Quiz' – an interesting checkup as to just how much we might choose to be 'children of light':

1. If you found a wallet with $1,500, would you give it to the owner if no one knew you found it?

2. If you could advance yourself unfairly, would you do it if no one would ever find out?

3. If the bus driver failed to collect your fare, would you voluntarily pay it?

4. If there were no locks on any house, store or bank, would you take anything if no one found out?

5. If your business partner died, would you pay his relatives their fair share, if you didn't have to?

6. If you were an employer, would you hire yourself at your salary?

7. If you were an employer, would you like to be working for yourself?

8. If you are a parent, would you like to be the child of a parent like you?

9. If you had a choice, would you like to live in a community of people working in church, civic and community affairs like you do?

10. If you had to live with someone just like you for the rest of your life, would you count it a privilege?[32]

I am defeated, and
know it, if I meet any
human being from
whom I find myself
unable to learn
anything.

*Let the wise listen and add to their learn-
ing, and let the discerning get guidance.*
Proverbs 1:5 NIV

Carlos Romulo, the former president of the Philippines, won an oratorical contest in the Manila high school he attended as a young man. His father was puzzled, however, when he saw his son ignore the congratulations of one of the other contestants. As they left the auditorium he asked, 'Why didn't you shake hands with Julio?'

Carlos said, 'I have no use for Julio. He was speaking ill of me before the contest.' The father put his arm around his son and said, 'Your grandfather used to tell me that the taller the bamboo grows, the lower it bends. Remember that always, my boy. The taller the bamboo grows, the lower it bends.'

Every person has something to teach us – not only those who are experts in their fields or tell us what we want to hear. Each person is a living encyclopedia of ideas, insights, facts, experiences and opinions.

A woman once advised a new employee: 'Fifty per cent of the people in this organisation will teach you what to do and the other fifty per cent what not to do. It's your challenge to figure out which per cent goes with which person.' Even if a person doesn't have a good example for you to follow, you can always learn from him or her what *not to do*!

Honesty is the first chapter of the book of wisdom.

Do things in such a way that everyone can see you are honest through and through.
Romans 12:17 TLB

The editor of the 'wedding and engagement' section of a local newspaper grew tired of hearing
from the town's citizens that she always embellished
her reports of parties and celebrations. She decided
that in the next issue she was going to tell the *truth*
and see if she had greater favour with the readers.
She wrote the following item:

'Married – Miss Sylvan Rhodes and James Collins,
last Saturday at the Baptist parsonage, by the Rev J.
Gordon. The bride is a very ordinary girl, who doesn't
know any more about cooking than a jackrabbit and
never helped her mother three days in her life. She is
not a beauty by any means and has a gait like a duck.
The groom is an up-to-date loafer. He has been living
off the old folks at home all his life and is now worth
nothing. It will be a hard life.'

We may not always need to be so brutally 'honest'
in telling the truth! Truth, after all, is ultimately
known only by God – who alone has the ability to see
into the hearts of men and women and know everything involved in any situation or relationship.
Rather, we should be honest in expressing our hopes
for another person's best welfare and success. That is
a truth everybody loves to hear.

God always gives His best
to those who leave the
choice with Him.

Blessed be the Lord,
Who daily load us with benefits,
The God of our salvation!
Psalm 68:19 NKJ

Author Elisabeth Elliot writes in *A Lamp for My Feet* about a game she played as a young girl. She writes, 'My mother or father would say, "Shut your eyes and hold out your hand." That was the promise of some lovely surprise. I trusted them, so I shut my eyes instantly and held out my hand. Whatever they were going to give me I was ready to take.' She continues, 'So should it be in our trust of our heavenly Father. Faith is the willingness to receive whatever He wants to give, or the willingness not to have what He does not want to give.'[33]

If your prayers aren't answered in the way you expect them to be, there may be a good reason! Several months before Christmas, Jared begged his mother to buy him a new bicycle just like his friend's – and he had to have it now. His mother was a single mum, however, and there was no extra money for a new bicycle until Christmas.

Jared's friend generously lent him his bicycle to ride and the longer Jared rode it, the more he realised it really wasn't the right bicycle for him. For one thing, it didn't have the racing brakes he wanted.

How often do we think God has forgotten us, when He's merely giving us time to understand what we really want and bringing us His best?

A lot of people mistake
a short memory
for a clear conscience

*So I strive always to keep my conscience
clear before God and man.*
Acts 24:16 NIV

In the 1980s a man drove by the farm of Mrs John R. McDonald. A sudden gust of wind caught his black derby hat and whirled it onto the McDonald property. He searched in vain for the hat and finally drove off bareheaded.

Mrs McDonald found the hat and for the next forty-five years various members of her family wore it. Finally the old derby was beyond repair, completely 'worn out'. It was at that point Mrs McDonald went to the local newspaper and advertised for the owner of the hat. She noted in her ad that while the hat had been on the *heads* of the menfolk in her family, the hat had been on her *conscience* for forty-five years!

Is something nagging at your heart today – an awareness that you have committed a wrong against another person, or a feeling that something has gone amiss in a relationship? Don't ignore those feelings. Seek to make amends. The sooner you do, the easier you'll find reconciliation or restoration – and the easier you'll find your rest at night.

A guilty conscience is a very heavy load to carry through life – one for which Jesus died on the cross. He did His part; now you do yours and obtain the freedom and peace He purchased for you!

Faith is not belief without
proof, but trust
without reservation.

*I know whom I have trusted, and I am
sure that he is able to keep safe until that
Day what he has entrusted to me.*
2 Timothy 1:12 GNB

During the terrible days of the Blitz in World War II a father – holding his young daughter by the hand – ran from a building that had been struck by a bomb. In the front garden was a large hole left by a shell explosion several days before. Seeking shelter as quickly as possible, the father jumped into the hole and then held up his arms for his young daughter to follow.

Terrified by the explosions around her and unable to see her father in the darkness of the hole, she cried, 'I can't see you papa!'

The father looked up against the sky that was lit with white tracer lights and tinted red by burning buildings and called to his daughter, who was standing in silhouette at the hole's edge, 'But I can see you, my darling. Jump!'

The little girl jumped . . . not because she could see her father, but because she trusted him to tell her the truth and to do what was best for her.

We may not be able to discern clearly where it is our Heavenly Father is leading us, but we can trust it is to a good place. We may not know what God has 'up His sleeve', but we can trust His arms to be everlasting.

A day hemmed in prayer is less likely to unravel.

Pray about everything; tell God your needs and don't forget to thank him for his answers. If you do this you will experience God's peace . . . His peace will keep your thoughts and your hearts quiet and at rest.

Philippians 4:6,7 TLB

It was 2.00 a.m. when a weary traveller landed in Tahiti. Her flight from Hawaii had been a turbulent one, causing a delay in her arrival on the island. The stormy skies also meant her connecting flight to a nearby island was cancelled, forcing her to make plans to spend at least a day near the airport. An hour later, she found herself standing with her luggage in a small but clean motel room, totally exhausted after more than twenty-four hours of travel. Her mind, however, refused to stop racing with concern about whom to call and what to do.

The woman was on a short-term missionary trip to help set up a clinic in a remote South Seas island. Now she was beginning to wonder if she had heard God correctly! At that hour, and as weary as she was, she felt alone at the edge of the world. Glancing down at her watch, she saw it read 11.00 a.m. – the time her Bible Study group had said they would be in prayer for her. *They're praying right now!* she thought, and suddenly, she felt deep peace and comfort. Within minutes, she was sound asleep.

When you are feeling as if you are about to unravel inside, turn to prayer. The travel route of prayer is never misdirected or put off schedule – nor is it dangerous! On the contrary, prayer gives peace and helps us avoid danger.

When you flee temptations don't leave a forwarding address.

*Now flee from youthful lusts,
and pursue righteousness, faith, love
and peace, with those who call on the
Lord from a pure heart.*
2 Timothy 2:22 NASB

Sally was trying desperately to save all the pennies she could for the doll's pram she wanted to buy. She was turning in aluminium cans, offering to do extra chores . . . anything to make a few more pennies a week.

One night, as she was saying her bedtime prayers, her mother overheard her say in great earnest, 'O Lord, please help me to save my money for the doll's pram in Mr Brown's shop window. It's so beautiful and I want it so much. It's just right for my doll. And I'd be sure to let my friends play with it too.'

Pleased at her daughter's prayer, Sally's mother was startled to hear the final line of the prayer. 'And please God, don't let the ice cream man come down our street this week!'

Just as we are each unique in our talents, abilities, background and experiences, we are also unique in what tempts us. What is tempting to one person may not be at all tempting to another.

Although the enemy of our souls knows our weak points, we know our Strength – Jesus. As we stick close to Him, when temptation comes, we can draw on His strength to turn from it.

Always say yes to Jesus, and saying no to temptation will become easy!

A coincidence
is a small miracle
where God
prefers to remain
anonymous.

Who can put into words and tell the
mighty deeds of the LORD? Or can show
forth all the praise [that is due to Him]?
Psalm 106:2 AMP

Victor Frankl was stripped of everything he owned when he was arrested by the Nazis in World War II. He arrived at Auschwitz with only his manuscript – a book he had been researching and writing for years – sewn into the lining of his coat. Upon arrival, even that was taken from him. He later wrote, 'I had to undergo and overcome the loss of my spiritual child . . . It seemed as if nothing and no one would survive me. I found myself confronted with the question of whether under such circumstances my life was ultimately void of any meaning.'

Days later, the Nazis forced the prisoners to give up their clothes. In return Frankl was given the rags of an inmate who had been sent to the gas chamber. In the pocket of the garment he found a torn piece of paper – a page from a Hebrew prayer book. On it was the foremost Jewish prayer, 'Shema Yisrael' which begins, 'Hear, O Israel! The Lord our God is one God'.

Frankl says, 'How should I have interpreted such a "coincidence" other than as a challenge to live my thoughts instead of merely putting them on paper?' He later wrote in his classic masterpiece, *Man's Search for Meaning*, 'He who has a *why* to live for can bear almost any *how*.'[34]

Sometimes the Lord
calms the storm;
sometimes He lets
the storm rage
and calms His child.

*And the peace of God, which transcends
all understanding, will guard your hearts
and your minds in Christ Jesus.*
Philippians 4:7 NIV

In *Especially for a Woman,* Beverly LaHaye writes about how upset she was when her husband, Tim, told her he wanted to take flying lessons. Her quick response was, 'I think you're foolish! Why would you want to get into a plane with only one engine?'

Tim asked her to pray about the matter, but she writes, 'I started right off giving God my opinions and drawing my own conclusions. My fear . . . was controlling me.' Tim suggested, 'Be open with the Lord . . . Let Him know you're afraid of flying, but that you're willing to be changed if that's what He would have.'

Beverly did just that. Tim took flying lessons, and repeatedly she committed her fears – and their lives – to the Lord.

Years later she was a passenger in a commuter plane that was caught in a storm. As the plane bounced in the sky, the LaHaye's attorney – normally a very calm man – felt sure they were going to crash. Then he looked over and saw that Beverly was asleep! He asked her later, 'How could you sleep so peacefully?'

Beverly responded, 'It has to be God. Only He could have brought me from that crippling fearfulness . . . to a place where I could fly through such a storm and be at peace.'[35]

The past should be
a springboard
not a hammock.

One thing I do, forgetting those things
which are behind and reaching forward to
those things which are ahead.
Philippians 3:13 NKJ

Many people are good starters but poor finishers. When the going starts getting tough they listen to the little imp on their shoulder that whispers, 'You can't do it' and 'You'll never make it'. Many others do not even start.

What we must realise is that while 'doing something' requires a risk, so does 'doing nothing'. The risk of action may be failure, but the risks of a failure to act can be stagnation, dissatisfaction and frustration . . . even loss to an evil enemy.

The story of the covered wagon crossing the plains toward the Golden West began with a song:

The Coward never started;
The Weak died on the way;
Only the Strong came through!

That's the way it is in life. But strength does not refer only to physical strength. True strength flows from the strong spirit – a spirit made powerful by a close relationship with God. He gives us the will to succeed, the dreams that will not die and the wisdom to turn any evil into a blessing.

Lean on God for direction and keep leaning on Him for the wisdom and courage to finish what you begin!

The teacher asked the pupils to tell the meaning of loving kindness. A little boy jumped up and said, 'Well, if I was hungry and someone gave me a piece of bread that would be kindness. But if they put a little jelly on it, that would be loving kindness.'

Praise the Lord, O my soul . . .
[who] crowns you with love and
compassion, who satisfies your desires
with good things.
Psalm 103: 1,4,5 NIV

Kindness provides a house, but love makes a home.

Kindness packs an adequate packed lunch, but love puts a note of encouragement inside.

Kindness provides a television set or computer as a learning aid, but love controls the remote control and cares enough to insist a child 'sign off'.

Kindness sends a child to bed on time, but love tucks the covers around a child's neck and provides a goodnight hug and kiss.

Kindness cooks a meal, but love selects the 'your favourite foods' menu and lights the candles.

Kindness writes a thank-you note, but love thinks to include a joke or photograph or bookmark inside the envelope.

Kindness keeps a clean and tidy house, but love adds a bouquet of fresh flowers.

Kindness pours a glass of milk, but love occasionally adds a little chocolate sauce.

Kindness is doing what is decent, basic, courteous and necessary for an even, smooth and gentle flow of life.

Love is taking the extra step to make life truly exciting, creative and meaningful. Love is what makes things special.

Laughter is a
tranquilliser
with no side effects.

A merry heart does good, like medicine.

Proverbs 17:22 NKJ

Norman Cousins was once asked by a group of physicians to meet with cancer patients at a hospital. He told how he had lost a quarter in a pay phone. 'Operator,' he said, 'I put in a quarter and didn't get my number.' She said, 'Sir if you give me your name and address, we'll mail the coin to you.'

He recited a full and long litany of all the steps and procedures and expense involved in returning his coin that way and concluded, 'Now, operator, why don't you just return my coin and let's be friends?'

She repeated her offer and then asked if he had pushed the coin-return plunger. He hadn't but when he did, the phone box spewed out close to four dollars worth of change!

The operator said, 'Sir, will you please put the coins back in the box?' Cousins replied, 'If you give me your name and address I will be glad to mail you the coins.'

The patients exploded with cheers as Cousins told his story. Then one of the physicians asked, 'How many of you came into this room in pain?' More than half raised their hands. 'How many of you in the past few minutes had less or no pain?' All nodded 'yes'.

Laughter – it's one of the best pain medications ever!

God never asks about
our ability
or our inability –
just our availability.

I heard the voice of the Lord, saying,
Whom shall I send, and
who will go for us?
Then said I, Here am I; send me.
Isaiah 6:8 AV

One of the items in Ripley's *Believe It or Not* is a picture of a plain bar of iron. It is valued at $5. The same bar of iron has a far different value, however, if it is fashioned into different items.

- As a pair of horseshoes, it would be worth $50
- As sewing needles, it would be worth $5,000
- As balance springs for fine Swiss watches, it would be worth $500,000.

The raw material is not what is important. What's important is how raw material is developed!

Each of us has been given talents and abilities – some have received more, others less, but all have received something as a unique gift from God. As Christians, we also enjoy spiritual gifts which flow from the Holy Spirit of God.

The value of these raw materials, however, is a moot point unless we develop and use our talents, abilities and spiritual gifts as a force for divine good in this world.

If you don't know what your abilities and gifts are, ask God to reveal them to you. Then ask Him to show you what He wants you to do with them. Your happiness and success in life will be found in fulfilling His plan for your life.

Whether you think you can
or think you can't
you're right.

As he thinks in his heart, so is he.
Proverbs 23:7 NKJ

Anew prison was built in British Columbia to replace the old Fort Alcan prison that had been used to house inmates for hundreds of years. After the prisoners were moved into their new quarters, they became part of a work crew to strip the old prison of lumber, electrical appliances and plumbing that might be reused. Under the supervision of guards, the inmates began tearing down the old prison walls.

As they did, they were shocked at what they found. Although massive locks had sealed heavy metal doors and two-inch steel bars had covered the windows of the cells, the walls of the prison had actually been made out of paper and clay, painted to resemble iron! If any of the prisoners had given a mighty heave or hard kick against a wall, they might easily have knocked a hole in it, allowing for escape. For years, however, they had huddled in their locked cells, regarding escape as impossible.

Nobody had ever *tried* to escape because they *thought* it was impossible.

Many people today are prisoners of fear. They never attempt to pursue their dreams because the thought of reaching them seems impossible. How do you know you can't succeed if you don't try?

The best way
to cheer yourself up
is to cheer up
somebody else.

Give, and it shall be given unto you.
Luke 6:38 AV

The grief-stricken mother sat in a hospital room in stunned silence, tears streaming down her cheeks. She had just lost her only child. She gazed into space as the sister asked her, 'Did you notice the little boy sitting in the hall just outside?' The woman shook her head no.

The nurse continued. 'His mother was brought here by ambulance from their poor one-room apartment. The two of them came to this country only three months ago, because all their family members had been killed in war. They don't know anyone here.

'That little boy has been sitting outside his mother's room every day for a week in the hope his mother would come out of her coma and speak to him.'

By now the woman was listening intently as the nurse continued, 'Fifteen minutes ago his mother died. It's my job to tell him that, at age seven, he is all alone in the world – there's nobody who even knows his name.' The nurse paused and then asked, 'I don't suppose you would tell him for me?'

The woman stood, dried her tears and went out to the boy.

She put her arms around the homeless child. She invited him to come with her to her childless home. In the darkest hour of both their lives, they became lights to each other.

Failure isn't falling down.
It's staying down.

Though a righteous man falls seven times,
he rises again.
Proverbs 24:16 NIV

In 1991 Anne Busquet was General Manager of the Optima Card division of American Express. When five of her 2,000 employees were found to have hidden $24 million in losses, she was held accountable. Busquet had to face the fact that, as an intense perfectionist, she apparently came across as intimidating and confrontational to her subordinates – to the point they were more willing to lie than to report bad news to her!

Busquet lost her Optima job, but was given a second chance by American Express: an opportunity to salvage one of its smaller businesses. Her self-esteem shaken, she nearly turned down the offer. Then she decided this was her chance to alter the way she related to others. She took on the new job as a personal challenge to change.

Realising she had to be much more understanding, she began to work on being more patient and listening more carefully and intently. She learned to solicit bad news in an unintimidating way.

Four years after she was removed from her previous position, Anne Busquet was promoted to be an executive vice-president of American Express.

Failure is not the end; it is a teacher for a new beginning and a better life!

Nobody can make you feel inferior without your consent.

I am fearfully and wonderfully made.
Psalm 139:14 AV

Three women, a psychologist, an engineer and a theologian, were on a hike when they came upon an unlocked cabin deep in the woods. Receiving no response to their knocks, they went inside to find one room, simply furnished. Nothing seemed unusual except that the large, potbellied, cast iron stove was hung from the ceiling, suspended in mid-air by wires.

The psychologist said, 'It is obvious this lonely trapper has elevated his stove so he can curl up under it and experience a return to the womb.' The engineer responded, 'Nonsense! This is thermodynamics! He has found a way to distribute heat more evenly in his cabin.' The theologian interrupted, 'I'm sure this has religious meaning. Fire "lifted up" has been a religious symbol for millennia.'

As the three debated, the cabin owner returned. The hikers immediately asked him why the stove was hung by wires from the ceiling. He replied succinctly, 'I had plenty of wire, but not much stove pipe.'

Others may try to second-guess your motives, downplay your ideas, or insult you, but only you know why you do what you do, what you think and feel and how you relate to God.

Stay true to who you are in Christ Jesus!

Acknowledgements

Ruth Bell Graham (6), Mother Teresa (8, 46, 250), Jean Hodges (10), George M. Adams (14), Glen Wheeler (16), Helen Pearson (20), Joseph Addison (22), Cyrus (24), Henry Ward Beecher (26), G.W.C. Thomas (32), Betty Mills (34), Josh Billings (36, 246), Thackery (38), Joyce Heinrich and Annette La Placa (40), Joyce Earline Steelburg (42), St. Basil (44), Catherine Graham (76), Lillian Dickson (78), Cevantes (80), Sebastian-Roche (82), Mark Twain (86, 214, 222), William James (88), Zig Ziglar (92), William Feather (94), Bill Cosby (96), Charles Dickens (98), Euripedes (102), Martin Luther King Jnr (104), William Carey (106), Benjamin Franklin (108), Dennis Waitley (114), Mary Gardner Brainard (118), Walt Disney (120), Arnold H. Glasgow (206), Mort Walker (208), Richard Exley (210), John Newton (216), Mark Steele (218), Olin Miller (228), Joseph P. Dooley (234), June Henderson (242), Dr John Olson (244), Reverend Larry Lorenzoni (254), James Howell (256) Ralph Waldo Emerson (258), Charles H. Spurgeon (264), George Herbert Palmer (266), Thomas Jefferson (268), Jim Elliot (270), Doug Larsen (272), Elton Trueblood (274), Ivern Ball (284), Merceline Cox (288), Henry Ford (292), Mary Pickford (296), Eleanor Roosevelt (298).

Notes

1. *Words to Live By*, Mother Teresa (Notre Dame, IN: Ave Maria Press, 1983) pp 55, 59.
2. *Especially for a Woman*, Anne Kiemel Anderson (Nashville, TN: Thomas Nelson Publishers, 1994) p 42.
3. *Illustrations for Preaching and Teaching*, Craig Brian Larson, ed. (Grand Rapids, MI: Baker Books, 1993) p 119.
4. 'That's What Friends Are For,' by Jane Gross, *Ladies Home Journal*, July 1995, p146.
5. *Family Circle*, September 1, 1995, p 114.
6. *Little House in the Ozarks*, Laura Ingalls Wilder (Nashville, TN: Thomas Nelson Publishers, 1991) p 36.
7. *People*, March 20, 1995, pp 87–88.
8. *A Closer Walk*, Catherine Marshall (London: Hodder & Stoughton, 1987).
9. *Dakota*, Kathleen Norris (New York, NY: Houghton Mifflin, 1993) p 18.
10. *TV Guide*, July 22, 1995, p 29.
11. 'Anatomy of a Champion,' George Sheehnan, *Runner's World*, May 1993, p 18.
12. *Learning to Forgive*, Doris Donnelly (New York, NY: Macmillan Publishing, 1979) pp 24–25.
13. *Newsweek*, April 24, 1995, p 150.
14. *Let Me Illustrate*, Albert P. Stauderman (Minneapolis, MN: Ausburg Press, 1983) p 104.
15. 'Of Love and Loss,' Jennet Conant, *Redbook*, October 1994, p 82.
16. *Illustrations for Preaching and Teaching*, Craig Brian Larson, ed. (Grand Rapids, MI: Baker Books, 1993) p 200.
17. *Decision*, September 1995, p 4–5.

18. *Little House in the Ozarks*, Laura Ingalls Wilder (Nashville, TN: Thomas Nelson Publishers, 1991) p 103.

19. 'Signs and Wonders,' John Garvey, *Commonweal*, April 22, 1994, p 10.

20. 'By Faith Not Sight,' Ruth A. Morgan, *Encyclopedia of 7700 Illustrations*, Paul Lee Tan, ed. (Rockville, MD: Assurance Publishers, 1979) p 404.

21. 'I know Something Good About You', *Knight's Master Book of New Illustrations*, Walter B. Knight (Grand Rapids, MI: Eerdmans Pub. Co, 1956) pp 174–175.

22. 'Disaster Weddings and How Couples Coped,' Barbara Rachel Pollack, *Redbook*, August 1995, p 102.

23. *Growing Strong in the Seasons of Life*, Charles Swindoll (Portland, OR: Multnomah Press, 1983) p 100.

24. 'Mottoes', Kalends, *The New Speaker's Treasury of Wit and Wisdom*, Herbert V. Prochnow, ed. (New York, NY: Harper and Row, 1958) p 290.

25. *Little House in the Ozarks*, Laura Ingalls Wilder (Nashville, TN: Thomas Nelson Publishers, 1991) p 68.

26. Author and title of poem unknown. Found in *Speaker's Encyclopedia of Stories, Quotations and Anecdotes*, Jacob M. Braude (Englewood Cliffs, NJ: Prentice-Hall, 1955) p 307.

27. Story from *Illustrations Unlimited*, James Hewett, ed. (Wheaton, IL: Tyndale House Publishers, 1988) pp 131–132.

28. *Illustrations for Preaching and Teaching*, Craig Brian Larson, ed. (Grand Rapids, MI: Baker Books, 1993) p 97.

29. Ibid p 187.

30. *It's My Turn*, Ruth Bell Graham (Minneapolis, MN: Grason, 1982) p 110.

31. 'Janette Oke: Pioneer Novelist', Nancy McGough, *Homelife*, November 1995, pp 12, 14–15.

32. 'A Character Quiz', Herbert V. Prochnow, *The Speaker's Book of Illustrations*, Herbert V. Prochnow, ed. (Grand Rapids, MI: Baker Book House, 1960) p 100.

33. *A Lamp For My Feet*, Elisabeth Elliot (Ann Arbor, MI: Servant Publications, 1987) p 52.

34. *Illustrations for Preaching and Teaching*, Craig Brian Larson, ed. (Grand Rapids, MI: Baker Books, 1993) pp 250–251.

35. *Especially for a Woman*, Beverly LaHaye (Nashville, TN: Thomas Nelson, 1994) pp 253, 263.

Other titles in the *God's Little Devotional Book* series published by Eagle are:

God's Little Devotional Book for Everyone
(0 86347 234 6)

God's Little Devotional Book on Prayer
(0 86347 235 4)

God's Little Devotional Book for Couples
(0 86347 272 9)

God's Little Devotional Book for Kids
(0 86347 286 9)

God's Little Devotional Book for Mothers
(0 86347 284 2)

God's Little Devotional Book for Every Day
(0 86347 285 0)